TOMORROW'S CATHOLICS
YESTERDAY'S CHURCH

TOMORROW'S CATHOLICS
YESTERDAY'S CHURCH

*The Two Cultures of
American Catholicism*

EUGENE KENNEDY

Triumph™ Books
Liguori, Missouri

Published by Triumph ™ Books
Liguori, Missouri
An Imprint of Liguori Publications

Grateful acknowledgment is made for permission to reprint excerpts from:

"The Waste Land" from *Collected Poems 1909-1962* by T.S. Eliot. Copyright 1936 by Harcourt Brace Jovanovich, Inc., copyright © 1963, 1964 by T.S. Eliot. Reprinted by permission of Harcourt Brace Jovanovich, Inc., and Faber and Faber.

"The Road Not Taken" by Robert Frost, from *The Poetry of Robert Frost,* edited by Edward Connery Lathem. Copyright 1916 by Holt, Rinehart, and Winston and renewed 1944 by Robert Frost. Reprinted by permission of Henry Holt and Company, Inc.

Death Comes for the Archbishop by Willa Cather. Copyright 1927 by Willa Cather and renewed 1955 by the executor of the estate of Willa Cather. Reprinted by permission of Random House.

Myths to Live By by Joseph Campbell. Copyright 1968 by Viking Companion. Used with permission of Viking Penguin, Inc.

Originally published in 1988 by Harper and Row, Inc.

Library of Congress Cataloging-in Publication Data

Kennedy, Eugene C.
    Tomorrow's Catholics, yesterday's church : the two cultures of American Catholicism / Eugene Kennedy.
      p. cm.
    Originally published: New York : Harper & Row, © 1988.
    Includes index.
    ISBN 0-89243-580-1
    1. Catholic Church—United States—History—20th century. 2. Catholics—United States—History—20th century. 3. United States—Church history—20th century. I. Title.
    [BX1406.2.K447 1995]
    282'.73'09045—dc20   94-41663
                                     CIP

Contents

For
Joseph Campbell

Wisdom I have loved,
and sought her out from my youth . . .

If you were blind, there would be no sin in that.
"But we see," you say, and your sin remains.

JOHN 9:41

I came that they may have life and have it to the full.

JOHN 10:10

I will not apologize for my digressions.
Digressions are part of my plan.

HERODOTUS

Introduction

In the years since this book was first published, history has both sharpened and dulled its central thesis that two cultures exist side by side in American Catholicism: Culture One and Culture Two.

Culture One is the institutional church that religion reporters cover as if it were the whole church. It resembles the famous "red train" that bore Yesterday's church in the form of East Coast prelates and the apostolic delegate across the country to the Chicago Eucharistic Congress in 1926. In each city, as my mother told me of witnessing their passage through Syracuse, New York, these scarlet-robed princes appeared to receive the cheers of the Catholic people who gathered proudly, in a cloud of steam and a mist of cinders, for their blessing.

Culture One, its fittings pitted but still polished every morning, still carries church officialdom to work every day, along with its stage sets and its technicians. Culture One Catholics think this is the only trip in the world worth taking. At times they seem to believe that if they could sufficiently revise the timetable, people would at least come out to see it rattle by every day and perhaps start riding with them again.

Tomorrow's Catholics live, as they have for many years, in Culture Two, and do not even look up anymore when they hear the whistle blow. These men and women are too involved in expressing their lives of faith through their lives of work and family to be distracted by the bureaucratic local that passes through the back streets of their towns every day. The latter keeps itself going, like an old steam train, for its own sake, fed by memory and the chatter of buffs who are fascinated by gossip about rights of way and who the next conductor might be.

Culture Two Catholics do not disdain Culture One Catholics, nor do they feel the need to revolt against them. Culture Two Catholics know that they constitute the Catholic Church and are committed in personal and public ways to bringing the teachings of Jesus to bear in what social critics have come to call the postmodern world. These men and women are the harvest of Catholicism's extraordinary success in the United States. Within the span of a century, poor immigrants built churches, schools, and colleges that enabled large numbers of their descendants to become theologically sophisticated, leavening the work place, the professions, the arts, and politics with the yeast of their Catholic faith.

Culture Two Catholics are transformed people. They do not depend on the priest, the bishop, or the pope for the Catholic convictions that are well integrated into their personalities. Their indifference to the letters, meetings, or intra-institutional buzz about which bishop will "get New York" or who the next Holy Father might be mark them as individuals whose Catholicism is internalized.

That Culture Two exists and flourishes is beyond question. The edge of this insight has grown dull, however, because the sacramental sense of unity of these de-institutionalized Catholics is now taken for granted. There is nothing new or exceptional about it. Nonetheless, the leaders of Culture One do not know quite what to do about it or how to relate to it.

Most American bishops have been sensibly pastoral in their realistic assessment of the situation. They know that the institution, whose structural integrity they are charged to maintain, is not relevant to the lives of these believers—which puts them in a difficult position. These bishops are caught between a commitment to their vows to support official policies on the one hand, and a pastoral awareness of how insensitive certain official policies are on the other hand—such as the papal refusal to discuss the ordination of women. Caught as they are, these American bishops realize that their authority as teachers is weakened.

Pastoral bishops make room for these sincere and knowledgeable Catholics. The greatest danger, of course, is that such Catholics, free of dependence on Culture One, may become increasingly detached from the institution. The burden is not on Catholics of internalized faith to turn backward, but for the faltering institution—fumbling with irrelevancies as priests once did with their cassock buttons—must catch up with them.

The burden is clearly on the institutional church to become fully the *sacramentum mudi*, the great transcendent and transparent home of believers in which the sacraments rather than the regulations are the bread and wine of life. Yet the institution, headed by John Paul II, one of the greatest popes of all history, reflects divided attitudes. While John Paul II grasps and speaks heroically to the needs of a spiritually starved world on the brink of a new century, he also longs for and acts vigorously to restore a nineteenth century hierarchical, clerically dominated institution. That is yesterday's church and it will not do for tomorrow's catholics.

The institution, which is surely not to be mistaken for the essence of the church, is, in fact, filled with symptoms of its problems. Perhaps the most obvious—and least explored—is the corruption of the clerical state offenses committed by its members. Beneath these scandals, which lay Catholics have tolerated as generously and patiently as a kindly confessor, the culture is in decay.

The hesitancy of many bishops to look into the causes of this decay—indeed, the inability of the bishops to develop a national policy or to promote adequate research into the difficulty—suggests that they sense but do not wish to find confirmation of the fact that the clerical state has, for complex reasons, attracted and given cover and respectability to many psychologically immature and conflicted candidates. This problem has broken through because the formerly rigid defense of Culture One—the unquestioned support, for example, of the kind of Catholics who went out to see the red train pass by—has largely collapsed.

The purifying truth would bring freedom and offer a magnificent opportunity for the church to renew its official culture so that it matches and nourishes that of lay people. Yesterday's church could become tomorrow's church before we pass over the threshold of the next century. Right now, however, the bishops not only resist learning what they must know to reform the clergy but many are accepting and ordaining men whose psychological conflicts they overlook or discount in a time of a priest shortage.

That means that the official church continues to look back at yesterday. Furthermore, the collapse of this once great crimson-trimmed steam train of a culture is being accelerated by the doomed effort to restore hierarchical forms in the space/information age. The more bishops try to revive yesterday, the more they smother it to death, guaranteeing that they will inexorably be forced to deal with the corruption of the clerical state and the other symptoms of its moribund condition that they are denying or trying to postpone at the present time.

The Catholic Church possesses sufficient new life to let die the forms that once expressed it. The existence of a widespread and confident Culture Two is one of the guarantees that a resurrection of faith and form would follow. This should be regarded as a sign of hope rather than of contradiction. It is, in fact, the sign of *the* times.

EUGENE KENNEDY
January 1995

TOMORROW'S CATHOLICS
YESTERDAY'S CHURCH

PART ONE

THE PRESENT CONDITION
OF
CATHOLICS IN AMERICA

1

The Two Cultures
of American Catholicism
Notes Toward a Definition

*For we wrestle not against flesh and blood, but against prin-
cipalities, against powers, against the rulers of the darkness of
this world, against spiritual wickedness in high places . . .*
—Ephesians 6:12

O earth, earth, earth, hear the word of the Lord . . .
—Jeremiah 22:29

Two cultures struggle, as Jacob with the angel, within the consciousness of contemporary American Catholicism. The first rises from and
finds its concerns as well as its imaginative expression in the traditional institutional structures of the church in the United States. The
second, born out of the first, is far more diffuse in its cares and its
self-understanding, and is far less absorbed with the inner and outer
life of institutional Catholicism. Organically interrelated, these cultures are out of synchronization with each other; their varying con-
structions of the world generate the ambivalent feeling tone that has
marked American Catholicism in the quarter century that has passed
since Vatican Council II was convened.

They do not stand toe to toe as enemies, as the relationship of so-called right- and left-wing Catholics is sometimes characterized. They are not necessarily opposed to each other at all. But they are different in ways that may prove crucial for the future shape and direction of American Catholicism. The central question, barely asked much less answered, comes to this: Is the second culture of American Catholicism, whose members exert influence indirectly through their freedom from ecclesiastical control, subtly transforming the American Catholic Church in its own image and likeness?

I am using the word *culture* somewhat in the style popularized by the British novelist C. P. Snow when he distinguished between two outlooks, the scientific and humanistic, which he perceived as competitive and influential in the West. Culture, for Snow, was a broad term, related to the use of the same root word in *cultural anthropology,* the study of our development based on the significant human signs of a linguistic, psychological, and social nature that humans scratch everywhere as they make passage through life. These vessels brim with information about how men and women view themselves and the universe, what is important to them, and how they lead their lives.

In this book, *culture* means roughly the differing phenomenological views of religion, church, and world that can make two Catholics, kneeling next to each other in the same pew, quite different from one another. *Culture* here refers to the combination of elements that shape these differing ways of looking at and introducing religious order and meaning into the surrounding world. *Culture,* for my purposes, refers to the life environment that religious faith generates. So understood, religious cultures, when examined, instruct us about the many dimensions of belief, from the idea of God, understandings of sin and virtue, the spiritual and social authority of the preacher in the pulpit, to the remembered feelings of Christmas in a crowded church or of a rainy spring funeral or a steamy June wedding. Powerful moments in a religious culture, each of these, and landmarks, often enough, in a life story.

Consider the differences between the culture of American Catholicism and that of American Episcopalianism. These vary markedly, offering a shorthand definition of each culture in their salient features of social aspiration and standing. They are similar in religious belief but very different in their American enculturation. Believing in almost exactly the same creed, they have sharply different angles of vision toward America and easily distinguishable textures of religious experience. Consider the births, a few years apart in the nineteenth century, of men whose destinies would be intertwined in the twentieth.

Franklin D. Roosevelt was christened as an Episcopalian on May 20, 1882, in St. James's Chapel at Hyde Park by the Reverend Dr. Philander K. Cady. The very names fit wonderfully the high social class into which, despite some opium-smuggling ancestors, the future president of the United States was born. Episcopalianism was the religion of America's ruling class, the faith of many of its financiers, merchants, and jurists, a creed of the gentry, of the "upstairs" residents. Their maids and drivers were often Catholic, frequently Irish, the immigrant "downstairs" class out of and away from which Joseph P. Kennedy, born in East Boston on September 6, 1888, was determined to move. The Catholic newcomers seemed a threat to comfortable Protestant gentility; even Henry James looked balefully out at the immigrant crowds, finding these Europeans far less charming in America than he had found them in Europe itself. The differences between the Roosevelts and the Kennedys were, in many ways, symbolized by their theologically related but sociologically distinct religions.

Religion as encompassing culture denominates the world, naming the sacred realms, identifying the spiritual tests, and interpreting the mysteries. It also has plenty of room for childhood memories, as mine, for example, does, of voices outside church hawking, in dragged-out New York accents on sultry Sunday mornings, thirties radio priest Father Charles Coughlin's paper, *Social Justice*. A thick, rich slice of Depression-era Catholicism is served up with such a culture-specific recollection. So religion as an environment is Proustian in its evocative power, incarnating itself in dramatic events, such as a person's first confession, a new pope's first blessing from the loggia of St. Peter's, and even such seemingly minor remembrances as the softened sound of donations dropping into padded collection baskets, or the whisper of devotional candles extinguishing themselves in their own melting. They are skin, shell, and silver bowl holding the mystery of a faith powerful enough to infiltrate every crack and fissure of our human experience. Religion as culture begets this harvest of incidents, invests them with meaning, places them carefully, always within reach, in something like a collective unconscious. They constitute a display of the spiritual and sensual elements of our lifelong human experience with a specific denominational culture. We are, in good measure, what we believe.

Catholicism, despite widespread national differences, once appeared to be a powerful, univocal worldwide culture, bound together by the papacy, the Latin language, and a strict demand for obedience to its teachings and its teachers. That was the culture against which, for example, many artists, such as James Joyce and Eugene O'Neill, rebelled. Catholicism's influence emerged strongly in their work, for, although they could not be freely creative, they could not mine their unconscious undefensively inside a totally dominating and expertly controlling institution, neither could they easily shed the culture that shaped their literary imaginations. That culture's boundaries were closely guarded, so that those who willingly and consciously departed, by way of divorce, marriage outside the church, or artistic exile, would find casual reentry difficult if not impossible. Such persons might be shunned, for example, when returning to family funerals, mourned as if dead in life, the "fallen aways" whose social punishment was extreme and effective. The culture's borders were always open, however, to repentant sinners who returned, even at the last moment of their lives, seeking forgiveness and reconciliation, seeking, in a sense, the comfort of their home culture.

The American Catholic culture, once so extraordinarily powerful and unified that everybody over a certain age has almost identical memories of it, now houses at least two environments. It still possesses an unusual capacity to create a sense of family feeling among its members. Perceived by outsiders as a highly influential player in world affairs, the fulfillment of every sinister prophecy of such hate papers as *The Menace,* an institution to be measured carefully and approached with caution, the Catholic Church to insiders seems far more like an extended family in which anybody may show up and everybody may speak up. This comfortable sense is caught marvelously in theologian David Tracy's observation that "the only people not afraid of the Catholic Church are Catholics." That familial environment explains why, as writer Jimmy Breslin has said, "Nobody ever leaves the Catholic Church," and why, of all churches, it continues to be so lively and fascinating even to those who peer into its windows to see what is going on now. But American Catholicism, despite this remarkable sacramental aura, does not deliver one and the same experience to all its members anymore.

As but one example, the church's border membrane is far more permeable now. Excommunication and social exclusion hardly exist and would be ineffective in most cases even if they did. The church's awesome power to punish, to conjure up a sense that the possibilities of eternal bliss or eternal flame depend on the outcome of a teenager's battle with a sexual thought or feeling, has diminished considerably. Nearing the twenty-first century, the church no longer controls the floodgates of guilt. But that is only part of what has occurred. Something has happened of such a radical nature, and with such enormous implications for Catholicism, that the transformation must be examined, at least in a preliminary manner. It is clear that, although intimately interrelated, two cultures of Catholicism, pulling away from each other as the global continents once did, can now be observed. As with the drifting land masses, they are filled with signs of their common origin, and bear each other's outline as well as the other half of each other's forests, deserts, and subterranean treasures. But they grow more distinct as they move farther away from each other. They are the same, yes, but very different.

When a great American newspaper or magazine assigns its religion editor to do a story "on the Catholic Church," they invariably mean the first or the institutional culture. That is "the church" reported on, analyzed, speculated about almost endlessly, frequently with an emphasis on the challenge to established authority that is implicit in some recent occurrence. An example is the Vatican's 1986 disciplinary actions against Seattle Archbishop Raymond Hunthausen for supposed deviance from orthodoxy in administering his diocese. Many of his pastoral initiatives, such as allowing DIGNITY, the homosexual Catholic support group, to have Mass in his cathedral, were hardly novel, since they were repeated in dioceses all over the country. His central difficulty lay in his threat to institutional rather than pastoral principles.

So, too, with Father Charles Curran, the moral theologian barred from teaching at Catholic University in Washington, D.C. The crucial issue was not so much what he taught, for he was, in fact, supported by seven hundred fellow theologians in his carefully nuanced reflections about birth control and homosexuality. The real problem was that, in the judgment of Roman officials, he *dissented* from what they described as the authoritative teaching of the church. If his theology was acceptable among his orthodox peers, then his offense was institutional rather than doctrinal in nature. He shares this offense with many distinguished thinkers of previous times, including Galileo, who was rehabilitated only a few years ago through the same Roman institutional agencies that once condemned him and are currently responsible for the censuring of Father Curran.

The First Culture emphasizes, stands by, and works diligently to protect the institution and its lines of control over the church at large. *Institutionality* might be a word well added to the list of the distinguishing characteristics (one, holy, catholic, and apostolic) that the church has traditionally claimed for itself. Why not? the commonsense questioner asks; after all, the church *is* an institution. The institution is a temporal, phenomenally fixed medium for realities that transcend its structures as the sun does a solar battery or a magnifying glass. The church is, in fact, essentially a mystery, in whose proclamation and service the institution finds its sole justification. This insight is the source of the tension between the two cultures of American Catholicism. Culture One is intrinsically dependent on the church *as institution* for its existence. Culture Two is intrinsically dependent on the church *as mystery* and only extrinsically dependent on it as institution.

Second Culture Catholicism is given little media coverage because, first, it is hard to report on a mystery, and, second, because it would be too much like reporting on ordinary life. Even those manifestations of religiously inspired behavior, such as the antiwar activities of the Berrigan brothers or the Sanctuary Movement to safeguard Central American exiles, that seem to stray beyond the limits of institutional Catholicism are actually closely related to and dependent on it for their effectiveness. They reveal the institution's presence in unexpected places, for they truly and explicitly represent it, proclaim its ideals, and derive their impact and gain attention because of their relationship with it. Charismatic Catholics, whose spontaneous and sometimes unintelligible style of prayer seems so markedly different from that of traditional Catholicism, are profoundly identified with Culture One, for they constantly seek the approbation of the institution and are at pains to prove that they belong firmly and fully to it.

Culture Two, as befits its essential grasp of the church as mystery, is, in a real sense, something else.

2

A Mighty Fortress Is Our God

Culture One

It may be the gift of ministry; it should be used for service . . . he who rules should exercise his authority with care . . .
—Romans 12:7, 8

For here we have no continuing city, but we seek one to come . . .
—Hebrews 13:14

The Roman Catholic Church is the only one we prefix with the . . .
—Lenny Bruce

America's dual Catholic cultures bear the same genetic material of Catholicism. The second grouping, especially because of the success of Catholic education, has moved out of the shadow of the official Catholicism that remains the absorbing, sometimes obsessing, First Culture environment. "Catholic education" refers broadly to the individual school systems as well as the colleges and universities established in America during the hundred years that reached from the middle of the last century to the middle of this one. This accomplishment was due largely through the small donations of working-class immigrant and second-generation Catholics. Reflecting their deeply held faith as well as their determination to identify and succeed in the host Protestant culture, this enormous undertaking, staffed by priests and religious men and women who descended from immigrants, was hugely successful in providing educational opportunities for Catholics. It had led them, by the last third of this century, not only to the White House but to large-scale, highly successful entrance into the professions, the arts, and business. By 1985, for example, almost one-third of the chief executive officers of the Fortune 500 companies were Catholics. This achievement flowed from the education that the First Culture made available through its energy and sacrifice for its children and grandchildren. The latter groups, well trained in theology as well as arts and science, became the citizens of Culture Two.

The media do not report on this large second, widely deployed wave of American Catholics because they are largely unaware of its existence or significance. No moral or journalistic fault is involved in this apparent neglect; it could not be otherwise in a church that talks about and to itself almost exclusively through the personnel of the First Culture, whose lives are inextricably involved with its concrete organizational reality.

Few if any Catholic commentaries or reflections have arisen independent of the programs, periodicals, or educational enterprises that flower densely in the primary culture of institutional Catholicism. That culture constitutes a self-maintaining economy, for it provides not only religious goods and services, but readily accessible consumers for them. The members of this kingdom speak to each other or to themselves all the time. This is not to say that its members are irrelevant, uninteresting, or unimportant, but to observe that they live, move, and have their being in a closed system in which the same ideas and concerns have been recirculating for generations.

Members of the First Culture may understand intellectually that large numbers of Catholics live beyond the pale of their own engrossing universe, but imaginatively they have difficulty in grasping it. Many of them have never ventured outside the busy, finely textured world of the First Culture. At times, they think they are outside it, when they are only in some portable incarnation of it, as, for example, at a Catholic educational or press convention. They remind one of the old joke about the walled-off part of heaven, about which a saved Protestant says, "That's the Catholic section. They think they're the only ones here."

Such observations are not meant to denigrate this extraordinary universe. They are meant, however, to point out that, vital and fascinating as it remains, it is spread as a relatively thin veneer on the massive substance of Second Culture Catholicism. Culture One is a crammed presence, a family album, a kitchen drawer, and an overflowing attic at the same time: it encompasses clergy, nuns, brothers, bishops, cardinals, colleges, universities, synods, con- claves, canon law, and dozens of other intriguing, and often endear- ing, embodiments of institutional Catholicism. This phenomenal environment is fascinating both in its aspirations and its flaws. It is augmented by phalanxes of laymen and women, including every- body from editors, writers, lawyers, and accountants, to pilgrimage tour planners and gravediggers, most of whom have lived their Catholicism within or at least in the shadow of the walls of the organized church.

The religious writers of the country "cover" Culture One not only because it is a clearly recognizable entity, but also because those they seek information from know its methods and its mores very well. I ought to know, for I am one of them. If Culture One sources say, as some have, that Pope John Paul II is trying to impose his sense of flame-tried Polish Catholicism on the United States, the headlines read "Catholics on Collision Course with Pope." If they argue the merits of celibacy, married or women priests, the impression is given that fifty million Catholics from coast to coast toss uneasily every night about such things. If they voice grave concern about a bishops' meeting, an ecclesiastical appointment, or some other event close to the sweet bone of institutional church life, these are projected as the universal cares of Catholic Americans. Nothing, of course, is further from the truth. Culture Two Catholics pay little, if any, attention to these staples of institutional concern.

This cleft between Catholicism's two cultures is not that of the "divided" Catholicism described in so many contemporary feature stories and television segments. Its existence is not neatly delineated by the differences between camps of so-called "Left-wing" and "Right-wing" Catholics. These latter groups belong largely to the same primary culture of American Catholicism, for what they share in common makes them, in a decisive way, more similar than dissimilar. Both groups are profoundly involved in the institutional Catholic Church; they are apparently dissimilar but both belong firmly to Culture One, sharing a strong interest in and commitment to the institutional church. These Catholics may identify themselves as locked in a battle for the church's soul, but this is a romantic exaggeration since both the Right and the Left are profoundly loyal to it and wish to preserve its glories, although with slightly different emphases, as an institution. Most of the people in these groupings are not only emotionally and spiritually but also economically dependent on the church *as a structure.* An analysis, for example, of those who attended the 1976 Call to Action conference revealed that more than 70 percent of the attendees who were suspected of being Left-wing Catholics were directly involved in institutional Catholicism. It was an illusion to presume that their intentions were other than to preserve and promote it.

The church *as institution* is the spine and central nervous system of Culture One. It may appear riven by disagreements but that does not shatter its unity or its integrity. As noted, its subgroupings may argue opposite sides of the questions that the media describe as significant in present-day Catholic life: celibacy, birth control, the possibility of married or women priests, a long agenda of social issues. But these groupings can only differ because they accept and embrace so much that is the same: the Church as an ongoing institutional presence in history, the pope, the bishops and clergy as its leaders and teachers, the familiar issues that seem natural to it because they are classically institutional in nature. Such issues persist in an unresolved state, not because they cannot be dealt with theologically—theologians, who know little about administration, do not have nearly as much difficulty with most of the controverted issues as administrators, who know little about theology, do—but because their resolution has so many political implications for the institutional church precisely as an institution. Modify the teaching on birth control, and administrative authorities would be forced to confront a more troublesome problem related to the institution's understanding of itself as a consistent and clear teacher over many centuries.

A notable threat to the institution's idea of itself arises if it is called upon to enlarge or transform its understanding or interpretation of a long-held doctrine. It hesitates, being innately cautious and, therefore, feeling theologically prudent, to modify a principle—its ban on birth control, for example—that also expresses so much about the value of life and the spirit of human generativity. And there is much that the institution can justify about such a stance. The institution resists because it does not yet fully grasp either the doctrinal, psychological, or sociological implications of such a change. But it also responds to its deep institutional instinct for self-preservation in refusing to reconsider the matter. In other words, institutional dynamics rather than theological reasoning govern much of the activity of Culture One. It senses that its first and most pressing task is to preserve itself rather than to place itself at risk.

The selection of bishops offers an excellent example of many of the issues that have so far been discussed. An extraordinary mythology encompasses the choice of bishops within Culture One. Research done on bishops by Dr. Frank Kobler at Loyola University of Chicago illustrates how firmly those chosen for the episcopal role believe that they were designated from all eternity to become "successors of the apostles." They fervently accept the idea that they have long been destined for special responsibilities. This profoundly buttressing belief works very well, for it is characteristic of bishops to give all of their energies to the church as an institution rather than the church as a mystery. Bishops are not, by their own admission, very good at mystery or at spiritual things, but they are chosen as *loyal administrators,* as men who will bind the organization together as a consistent, enduring presence in human affairs.

Very few American Catholic bishops display any artistic creativity; they are not lovers of ambivalence, as artists must be, and are chosen precisely because they are not so inclined. Whether from all eternity or not, the typical bishop is chosen as a man of good character and record who will work totally for the institution. For that reason, Pope John Paul II has instructed bishops *not* to submit, for appointment as bishops, any men who have *ever* voiced dissent on the issues of birth control, women priests, or celibacy. One must conclude that, whatever their other virtues, bishops are fundamentally Culture One Catholics, committed above all to institutional ends. That makes for a stable, if not very creative, college of episcopal leaders. They are the core members, as nucleus to cell, of Culture One.

Later, we will consider in greater depth why these particular issues —celibacy, birth control, women priests—are experienced as so threatening by the institutional church. What do they have in common, besides their obvious sexual reference, that has made these *the* questions that determine a person's loyalty and worthiness? These are the issues, *par excellence,* in Culture One, for it is in this setting that they are endlessly and inconclusively debated. Culture One seems obsessed, if not possessed, one way or the other, by these matters. These are, literally, very *telling* controversies, for they tell us that *control* is the central dynamic of institutional Catholicism.

Control comes from the medieval Latin *contrarotulus,* literally, *contra,* against or opposite, *rotulus,* little wheel. The root *ret* means to run or to roll and shows up in words as diverse as *rodeo, roulette,* and *control.* It is also the root of *rota,* the name, prefixed by *sacred,* given to that department of the Roman Curia that decides on petitions for annulments of Catholic marriages. We should not be surprised by this family reunion of meanings, for the Curia is determined to be the brake on anything that might get out of its control. Its members, keen institutionalists all, intuitively understand that power in the structure depends on controlling access to the clerical layer of the hierarchy as well as those areas of behavior in which human beings are most vulnerable, those related to sex and marriage, and which, therefore, allow them extensive control over women.

Curialists, no matter the rationalizations for their arguments, resist the admission of women to the priesthood, defend celibacy, and closely supervise the universe of sexuality because they thereby maintain for themselves the control which they apparently perceive to be threatened by women. This continuing dynamic in institutional history is a function of male bureaucratic behavior far more than of any divinely ordained arrangement. Healthy women sense very clearly the enormous opposition to their having any access to decision-making positions in the church; they appreciate that the underlying issue is power far more than it is authority. Culture One's ancient gnarled roots, entwined deep in the bone-strewn layers of lost and gone centuries, anchor it firmly even in the hurricane winds of modern times.

3

The Mystery of the
People of God

Culture Two

*Many are in high places, and of renown; but mysteries are
revealed unto the meek . . .*
                                                    —Ecclesiasticus 3:19

*I am convinced . . . that you are filled with goodness, that you
have complete knowledge, and that you are able to give advice
to one another. . .*
                                                    —Romans 15:14

Culture Two Catholics have no communal voice to match that of
their religious siblings in the first cohort of believers. Second Culture Catholics do not find themselves so intimately involved in the
institutional actions or debates, which, distant from their own experience, do not attract them. That is to say, such perennial controversies
as those centering on women priests and celibacy, with their deep,
complex, and inextricable connections with the structural underpin-
nings of the First Culture, do not have the same interest or force in
the Second Culture because these are not its ordinary concerns or
the moral and ethical issues that absorb its daily attention. The
Second Culture's existence does not depend on the preservation of

either celibacy or an all-male priesthood. Its extraterritoriality makes its mission, such as discerning at least the faint outlines of meaning in everyday life, and working with moral dignity in a materialistic and number-struck world, more socially and personally urgent than the institutionally oriented goals of the First Culture.

Culture Two Catholics are neither hostile nor indifferent to their faith. Unlike "cultural Catholics," who are tenuously and sometimes superstitiously attached to both living faith and bureaucratic institution, with little more than vague memories of a one-time connection with the church, Culture Two Catholics identify themselves deeply as Catholics, attend church regularly, accept and recite the creed, and acknowledge the pope and the clergy. They are not defined by their estrangement from or anger toward any of these. But they view the church as far less institutionally compelling or even attractive than do members of the First Culture. Institutionally, that grandly turreted compound resembles an ancestral castle from a bygone time and they feel that they are still part of the descendant family even though they no longer choose to live in its splendor-filled interior.

The lives of Second Culture Catholics are deeply attuned both spiritually and emotionally to the church as a sacramental source of interpretation and transmission of meaning, tradition, and teaching, as well as an agent of pastoral support and consolation. They are definitely not the unobservant Catholics in name only who have, like the poor, always been with the church; neither are they actively rebellious, nor do they stand in the front ranks of those described as dissidents. They are psychologically independent of the canonically erected, clerically layered, heroically envisaged church that appears, according to the papers and television, to be the only one that exists.

Second Culture Catholics do not hold their breath when a Synod of Bishops is held in Rome; they do not care much about who may succeed to some archiepiscopal vacancy in a powerful city such as Philadelphia, New York, or Los Angeles. They do not listen to supercilious discussions about whether purple should be replaced by blue as a liturgical color, and they cannot imagine that anybody, except the profoundly unreconstructed, would consider the latter as possessing religious significance. Culture Two Catholics do not follow the strictly ecclesiastical "news" whose buzz can be heard constantly in the pillared halls of the First Culture.

The daily rounds of Second Culture Catholics are simply not touched by the echoing, seemingly never adjourned discussions, such as those concerning birth control, celibacy, or women priests. Nor do they feel that their religious fervor or belief is tested by whether they side with either the Vatican or its critics on such questions. For them Catholicism is a way of life, and they have enough to do managing the problems of their everyday existence, taking care of the young and the old, as well as themselves. They are absorbed not by institutional issues but by the demands of the simplest virtues—faith, hope, and love—that are still literally and symbolically the breath of their days. They inhale and exhale the Spirit in their most important human activities, those crucial efforts that enlarge or diminish life in themselves and in all those whose destinies they affect.

They look to the church for support in carrying out their responsibilities to their families, and, in the work force and the professions, they expect that the church can speak to them with wisdom and encouragement about the great moral issues of the day. They expect that the church will comprehend tragedy and joy and that it will stand with them in both. But these are quiet Catholics whose lives are light years away from those of most of the priests who preach to them on Sundays. There are plenty of them out there. Many First Culture Catholics, enthralled and fulfilled by the institution, do not really understand that or how they exist.

The media continue to tell the story of Culture One as that of American Catholicism because they cannot, even with their finest observers and cameras, literally *see* the Second Culture as it functions in response to its own quiet but powerful dynamics. Culture One stories are actually reports from a way of life that is passing away. The present dimensions of institutional Catholicism are generally measured by Culture One members who use devices fashioned within and specifically for that culture. They note the depth and width of that which surrounds them, and which rises so majestically that it seems to constitute the "real" church. What else, they ask, would you measure? Almost all reported statistics on the Catholic Church in the United States reflect institutional rather than sacramental reality. Indeed, for many years the annual reports of all dioceses employed numbers as adequate measures of the spiritual health of the church. Listed, for example, were not only the number of baptisms and school enrollments but also the number of times the Eucharist was received in various parishes. This mathematical model of religious practice was also reflected in the "spiritual bouquet," a time-honored gift presented on suitable occasions. It consisted of a list of activities such as Masses attended, communions received, rosaries recited, and other greater and lesser prayers said for the beneficiary. While these signaled spiritual concern and largeness of heart, the use of quantitative measures reflected a kind of organizational bookkeeping of the spirit whose inherent incongruity seemed never to occur to anyone.

Even some social scientists so frame their inquiries that their results reflect a presumption that ordinary Catholics are consciously in conflict with the institutional church. Such surveys may, for example, report a "rejection of the authority of the Catholic bishops" by Catholics who have different convictions than their leaders about the morality of birth control and other questions of sexual ethics. One must examine this all-too-familiar story, and others like it, to see how the very statement of the issues and the phrasing of the questions reflect the tunnel vision of inveterate dwellers in the primary Catholic culture. In other words, such observations normally come from those bound up in the culture that is necessarily intensely focused on institutional matters, that universe in which the instrument of obedience is constantly being reshaped on the anvil of authority. This reflects the inquirer's preoccupation with potential conflicts with institutional authority that do not even enter the awareness of Second Culture Catholics.

Although research questions on sexual attitudes are now presented in a way that suggests a consciousness of liberal modernity, their roots are in the same narrowed organizational vision of life that once isolated sexual failings as practically the only raw material from which mortal sins could be manufactured. The range of subject matter has shifted very little, and contemporary inferences are still drawn from the hierarchical conning tower of a past age. Translating all life into the institutional language provides simplified subtitles for contemporary American Catholicism. This organizational set presumes that episcopal authority is ever central and consciously determinative in the lives of all Catholics. In real life, Culture Two Catholics are often too busy to notice what is playing at the long-running institutional festival. But they feel in no way actively alienated from the institutional church. They observe it, respect its leaders and official members, but they are not emotionally involved with or imaginatively dominated by it.

Indeed, Culture One gave birth to Culture Two, taught it powerful ideals, including the moral obligation of its members to believe and think for themselves. And so they have. They form their own consciences as they confront multiple daily choices; they exhibit a readiness to do this without necessarily perceiving themselves as rebels against the institutional order of the first culture. To act independently and responsibly cannot always be accurately depicted as a revolt against authority. Most people regard it as growing up.

To act otherwise would make them resemble young adults with their own growing families who refer every vital issue back to their own families of origin, never really leaving the universe of their nuclear families, composing every decision in terms of obeying or disobeying their own parents, seeing everything, not in terms of their present existential relationships to each other and to their children, but as tests of their loyalty to their mothers and fathers, to the customs and mode of authority from which common sense tells them they must actively move away to have healthy lives of their own. Just as most people do not think of every choice as yet another act in a never-resolved rebellion against the authority of their own parents, so Culture Two Catholics do not conceive their choices as episodes on a continuum of revolt against the pope, the bishops, their pastors, or ecclesiastical authority of any kind.

It may be shocking, even disappointing, for the administrators of Culture One to accept the fact that their presence is peripheral in the lives of most Catholics, that insofar as they move on a concrete, literalist plane, their shadows fall largely on their fellow citizens in the institutional church. They resemble learning psychotherapists who are surprised, but wiser, when they discover that their patients' apparent interest in and "love" for them, is really a transference phenomenon. That means that therapists are the objects onto which the patients project emotions that they actually have for *other* important persons in their lives.

For novice therapists, this first psychic bloodletting is profoundly educational. Through it, they learn that they have erroneously accepted all the attention of their patients as though it were actually directed toward them. The patients, in fact, weren't thinking about them at all. They were not as attractive, interesting, or compelling as these misunderstood compliments and advances led them to believe. They were not at the center of the patients' imagination, the object of their concern or passion. Accepting that, they perceive themselves more accurately, and they begin to appreciate the soundless depths of their patients and of the worlds, so different from their own, in which their true lives are led.

Something very similar is taking place in the American Catholic Church. Its leaders, much like the therapists of our example, have yet to understand that they are not the center of concern or attention of their people. While their pictures, columns, and schedules may dominate the diocesan newspapers, and while their activities are followed closely by the secular media, most American bishops are peripheral figures in the imaginations of even the best Catholics. Bishops and priests certainly were the center of attention at an earlier stage of the Catholic community's development in America, especially during the immigrant era, when these pastoral figures played such a significant role in identifying and fighting for the rights of largely unlettered believers. At that time the poor newly arrived

Catholics, seeking a toehold of their own in a suspicious Protestant culture, were proud to have their bishops live in houses as big as any governor's and to ride in cars as long as any mayor's. The bishop was a symbolic figure who strengthened the identity and self-esteem of Catholics.

As Catholics have advanced in America, their bishops have receded in their consciousness. They do not reject episcopal authority but they certainly do not accept official pronouncements automatically anymore. Only inside the first culture—and there perhaps only among persons intimately associated with institutional matters—do bishops command daily concern or interest. There is no harshness of mood in this transformation of the imaginative preoccupations of Culture Two. Bishops, much like learning therapists, will achieve the beginning of wisdom when they accept the fact that most Catholics aren't thinking about them at all.

4

Alpha and Omega

Alike and Different

*Abraham was the father of Isaac, Isaac the father of Jacob,
Jacob the father of Judah and his brothers . . .*
                                                    —Matthew 1:2

*Why did you search for me? Did you not know that I had to
be in my Father's house?*
                                                    —Luke 2:49

Culture Two Catholics are widely deployed, finding their center of
gravity in America at large rather than within the handsomely fenced
churchyard of ecclesiastical structure. They are not uninterested in
the church and they are delighted when, as in the life and work of
Pope John XXIII or Mother Teresa, it lights and warms a dark, cold
world. They are proud of Pope John Paul II as he strides, manfully
and confidently, on pilgrimages of peace across the globe. These
Catholics are impressed when their bishops leave institutional concerns behind them in order to address major societal problems. But
they are almost totally involved with their families and their work,
with troubles and challenges enough to excuse themselves from
paying much attention when the priest reads yet another letter from
the bishop at Sunday Mass.

Indeed, Culture Two Catholics, the beneficiaries of the enormous

achievements, particularly educational, of Culture One, display, in
their attitude toward religious structures and leaders, sentiments that
are healthy, unstudied, and profoundly Catholic. They reflect, unself-consciously, the sacramental thrust of Catholicism at its best, that
is Catholicism in love with art rather than law, Catholicism at home
in the world instead of embattled with it, Catholicism as the agent
of freedom, rather than only of control, for all that is profoundly
human. In a true sense, they are the dream realized of the great
theological and pastoral dreamers of the first culture.

Culture Two believers are, in the finest Catholic tradition, idealists
who are tolerant of human failure; they are not surprised by sin, and
they are ready to forgive. Reconciliation is a profound theme that
runs like a river through both cultures. There is a saving earthiness
to sacramental Catholicism. Culture Two Catholics, like Catholics in
general and despite the rise of Catholic Charismatics who favor
controlled spiritual emotion, underplay their practice of religion.
Faith for them is realized in a social context as much as in church,
and is marked by a largeness of heart rather than by the pinched
cheeks of austere and uncomforted piety. Culture Two responds to
the sacramental world proclaimed to it as the ideal by the teachers
and preachers of the mother culture. And its members have learned
how to deal, respectfully but without intimidation, with the many
incarnations of structural religion they encounter in their lives.

Catholics of this second grouping have an affectionate appreciation and tolerance of ecclesiastical figures. They have learned how
to handle them. They know how to wait out sermons; they understand, by a combination of intuition and long experience, what is
significant and what is not in the celebration of the Eucharist. This
universal feeling of being at home in their church marks Catholics
in a special way, and this overlapping generous spiritual kinship
allows the two cultures to intermingle without losing their separate
identities. They can tent together, to use a metaphor from the origins
of Christianity, for they share a powerful heritage. Yet, in the same
tabernacle, they look at themselves and at each other in remarkably
different ways. Gathered together, they can easily be distinguished

as citizens of the structure or members of something larger and less easy to define. And yet they recognize each other as members, some of the inner circle, some at large, of the same mysterious ecclesial reality. Indeed, in receiving each other they reveal a rich aspect— something of the many mansions of the gospel—of the mystery of the Catholic Church. Genuine mystery is almost always revealed, hardly ever proclaimed, and never self-consciously insisted upon.

Grace is not cheap or sentimental, the Catholic tradition recognizes, because there is no easy way to become human. The two cultures are bound together by a tragic appreciation of life. Nothing is more thoroughly Catholic than this feeling for the raveled edges of even the most noble lives or enterprises. Catholicism does not view religion as a resort area in which invisible hands trim the lawns and palms that stand in immaculate symmetry beneath cloudless skies. It provides instead a faith that matches the failure, death, and disappointment, the small and large hurts from which nobody is exempt. The soundings one takes of Catholicism are of living waters far deeper than the ringing framework of its aboveground institutional structures.

Culture Two Catholics see themselves as *the church,* not as an organization but as a *People of God.* They perceive Culture One as the administrator and servant of Culture Two, the governmental apparatus, necessarily highly organized and bureaucratic, whose sole function is to support and nourish their presence as *the mystery* of salvation at work in the world. The two cultures coexist despite these very different emphases. Indeed, many Culture One leaders realize that they compromise their own authority whenever they insist too much on laws that do not match the trustworthy life experience of Culture Two Catholics. Hence their emphasis on the pastoral approach in their dealing with them in recent years. One might also hypothesize that the pastoral language, heavily flavored with sacramental metaphor, is *the* common tongue that, even in different dialects, both cultures can understand.

The pastoral approach refers to a rich, humane, and sacramental appreciation of life, a solid middle ground between the lofty ideals of church teaching and the near misses that are so common in people's pursuit of them. One handles a situation pastorally not by completely ignoring the laws and regulations of the church but by applying them in an understanding manner. Pastoral service depends far more on the spirit than the letter of the law; it makes a passage through the drowning pool of bureaucracy and creates a genuine sacramental ambience of acceptance, forgiveness, and confirmation of available strength. It is well exemplified in the birth-control discussion, that chronically painful situation that is eased by bishops and priests who, while repeating the church's teaching faithfully, do not apply it with the rigid fervor that might alienate people further from their faith. The pastoral approach understands that people make incredible mistakes in choosing marriage partners and finds ways to use church law to serve the already suffering people involved. A pastoral approach meets people down in the valley of their experience rather than insisting that they climb some rocky pilgrimage mountain as the exhausting, knee- and heart-bleeding price of forgiveness or encouragement. The two cultures feel comfortable together in the pastoral aura of a sacramental church.

Culture Two's extraordinary embrace of the theological vision of Vatican II is one of its most distinguishing characteristics. It must, of course, be graciously admitted that Vatican II was the supreme function of the institutional church in this century. What else could an institution deliver as a gift except a meeting? Yet the council proved to be a long-delayed family gathering, and, therefore, the natural environment for the experience of sacramental mystery. Vatican II may be understood as an event wiser than the bureaucratic machinery that produced it, one that broke Culture One open to the Spirit and made possible its own internal reform, even at the level of law and procedure. Despite the compromise nature of its documents, Vatican II foreshadowed and made Culture Two Catholicism possible and inevitable.

Vatican II was a response to almost a century of ferment and intellectual activity, largely European in origin, in which the capacity to think freely, deeply, and with the help of current research tools was slowly and painfully regained. As we shall presently see, a fierce and unforgiving period of intellectual repression opened with the 1907 papal decrees against "Modernism," and only with great difficulty did Catholics find their way confidently back into the light of genuine scholarship. This was a major influence in shaping the attitudes toward the basic notions of faith, institution, authority, and obedience that have come to distinguish America's bicultural Catholicism. It was no accident that the first universal codification of canon law was achieved during this high cycle of institutional power. Indeed, it is fascinating to study the 1917 code, for practically its first subject matter was power, *potestas,* as it was to be understood and exercised within what it conceived to be the perfect hierarchically ordered society of the church.

Ironically, the very insistence on supervision and control that had marked Roman relations with the church in America had, through the enactments of the plenary councils at Baltimore, planted the seeds that would bloom in the enormous Catholic education system that was so influential in restoring intellectual ambition and freedom to American Catholics. The principle of Catholic primary schools was firmly established at that time. Amid the slowly developing colleges and universities, these elementary schools, whose success depended largely on the dedication of religious women, became the first teachers and shapers of a unifying American Catholic consciousness. They strengthened the importance and character of parish life (in many heavily Catholic dioceses, such as Brooklyn and Chicago, people signaled their place of origin with the name of a parish rather than of a neighborhood) and proved to be the source of the immense number of vocations that so solidified the institutional church in the United States.

Indeed, so formidable did this structure become and so large did it loom in the Catholic and national imagination that, despite the teaching on the Mystical Body of Christ, any noninstitutional concept of church seemed unthinkable. The will to build an enormous and well-supervised educational system led, however, to diminishing the bureaucratic control of thought by rehabilitating the intellectual life and encouraging people to think for themselves. Authoritarian Catholicism, in practice the effort to exercise excessive and often strangely motivated control over others, ultimately undermined itself by hastening the restoration of freedom and of genuine authority to the consciences of believers.

The present drop in what were once tightly and clearly defined as religious vocations is a symptom of the decline, not of faith, but of Culture One's power to control the psycho-social environment of its membership. What was broken was the power, not of faith but of guilt, to bind consciences to the dictates of the church to avoid eternal punishment and earn heavenly rewards. The psychology of vocations was deeply affected by this remarkable obsessive-compulsive quality of Catholic church life. Many people did not feel free to turn away from the emotional conviction that, no matter their own inner dispositions or ambitions, they *had* to accept and persevere in the call to the priesthood or religious life. Confessions were, as any priest experienced in hearing them can attest, marked not so much by the admission of major sins as the dealing with the questionable guilt of small faults. The gradual but pronounced lessening of the use of the sacrament of reconciliation, once better known as penance or, simply, confession, may be a signal that Catholics are employing better judgment about what is truly sinful and are not falsely accusing themselves about seeming spiritual imperfections. Better to have fewer people freely choose the seminary and religious life than to have hundreds respond out of an oppressive feeling of blind and compulsive duty.

Since there has been what can only be described as a boom in commitment to the works of ministry by large numbers of Catholics of every age, sex, and background, it is obvious that there is no real decline in the kind of faith needed for persons to give themselves to the work of the church. Now, however, it is no longer on the terms of Culture One but, rather, on those of Culture Two. The real problem for American Catholicism arose during the golden age of the institutional church, in which the priesthood and religious life attracted more candidates than bishops and superiors knew what to do with. Officials had to invent nonpastoral, nonsacramental jobs for priests and, as a result, they often ended up doing things far removed from pastoral ministry, sometimes spending their time in financial and administrative tasks that could easily have been performed by laypersons.

Psychological research done at Loyola University of Chicago on American priests and bishops in the 1970s revealed how powerfully influential the obsessive-compulsive dynamic, the demand of duty that could not be rejected without experiencing overwhelming guilt, was in shaping the interior sense of being called to a way of life that was most perfect and, therefore, nonrefusable, a common description of "having a vocation" during the period of strong institutional domination of Catholic life. These obsessive-compulsive tendencies were fostered by the Catholic culture of the time. There is nothing wrong with this; the obsessive-compulsive dynamic provides a reasonable explanation of many people's experience. By common account, in this research and in other explorations done subsequently, men and women felt compelled, as mentioned above, to enter seminaries and convents, to place their lives under the control of the institution. That the numbers of people who felt bound to do this declined as the control of the institution over conscience and will also declined is, therefore, not surprising. In a church whose members will have an increasing identification with Culture Two, we should expect fewer priests, more ministerial colleagues, and a better identity for both.

This same research, dovetailing with that done on such other mass bureaucracies as the armed forces, showed another price exacted from some of the most talented people who entered the priesthood. The most creative of them were not welcomed into the ranks of the bureaucracy precisely because *they were* creative. Hardly any truly creative person was ever appointed a bishop, and those who, like Bishop Fulton J. Sheen, finally were appointed to dioceses, were misfits, both unhappy and unsuccessful in carrying out the basically uncreative routine of administration. Far more commonly, creative people simply found their way into what were called "special assignments," activities related to the church but carried out on its margins. Father James Keller, founder of the Christophers, for example, was a creative person who finally developed a universe of activity that matched his genius as a leader and a fundraiser. It was routine for the creative to be shunted into areas where they could exercise their talents and not influence the bureaucratic soul of the institutional church.

Not every creative person ended up in happy circumstances. The loss to the institution, in its outright failure to understand or employ its creative personnel, is a cost seldom factored in when assessing the institutional church. The often-tragic price for creative persons who lived frustrated half lives—often thinking it was their own fault—has never been explored adequately. And what, we may ask parenthetically, does it mean when the leadership class of an organization must systematically rule out of its ranks all but those men whose doggedly obsessive relations with the institution are described, with the same poetic license given to course descriptions in a college catalog, as "loyalty"?

Culture Two Catholicism was clearly forecast in the vigorous lay movements and experimentation, especially in France and America after World War Two. Although then intimately tied to the institutional church, they manifested the resources of reflection and interest that inspired and offered a theological and scriptural foundation for the work of Vatican II. That was a council waiting to be called, and it took a man who had lived his ecclesiastical career largely outside of Rome—in Greece, Turkey, Romania, and France—to convoke it. Pope John XXIII, himself a quintessential product of the institution, a priest whose big heart expressed itself in traditional pieties, nonetheless proved to be the first holy father to understand the church as universal in nature rather than merely an extension of Western Europe. John may well be the patron saint of Culture Two because he anticipated, in his own life, its view of a world vaster than Rome.

In the United States, Culture Two members did not create themselves. Their lives come from the generativity of the institutionally oriented Catholicism from which, as growing offspring in a healthy family, they now distinguish themselves. Their readiness to move into the world with a consciousness of their being the church is already witnessed across the land in every diocese. Even a casual visitor may now observe liturgical participation by the laity that would have been considered, even immediately after Vatican II, advanced beyond even radical expectations. Laypeople perform *most* of the services, except for the celebration of the Eucharist, that were restricted to, and defined the daily activity of, priests a generation ago. Many of these laymen and laywomen are well beyond middle age and, even though they might not so describe themselves, are, operationally speaking, members of Culture Two.

They, and younger people, are the fulfillment, necessarily and perhaps reassuringly imperfect, of the vision and struggle of those institutionally bound Catholics who preceded, educated, and inspired them. But they are markedly different in their comprehension of the meaning of the church in the world. They realize in their own lives the great hope of heroic institutional Catholicism: to be bearers of the distinctive mystery of Catholicism as it places itself at the service of the world. Their Catholicism, a kind of orthodoxy outside institutional control, may well cause church structures to be transformed more rapidly than anyone might have anticipated. So, too, their hunger for sacramental spirituality as the hallmark of teaching authority will exert great pressure on church leaders. It would be sad, although certainly conceivable, if ecclesiastical leaders should, as almost a last resort, make more room for mystery in a less concretized religion in order to maintain institutional stability and to rehabilitate their own authority. This cannot, however, be done by edict or achieved through rote learning on their part, but only by a wholehearted return to the church's mystical tradition.

The official church cannot afford to lose contact with Culture Two. Ultimately pragmatic, the organization will eventually and inevitably make peace with its own people, emphasizing and implementing rather than insisting on a progressively less efficacious authoritarian style. In other words, the Catholic Church will, in the future, form itself increasingly around a Culture Two consciousness in order to survive and grow organically. The old arguments and seemingly deathless causes of Culture One—celibacy and the other death rattles of authoritarianism—will cease to be relevant and will, as a result, drop away naturally.

5

The Voice of the Catholic Is Heard in the Land

What American Catholics Say About Themselves

Many surveys have been conducted on America's Catholic population in recent years. When the results have been published in newspapers and magazines, they have almost always been accompanied by interpretations stressing the challenge to church authority that these attitudes seem to suggest. As we have noted, this tendency to present Catholics as not only disobedient but ready to mount the barricades in a rebellion against the pope and the bishops finds only faint and minor correlates in the actual behavior of American Catholics. Small groups, some on the Left and others on the Right, engage in vociferous, sometimes rude demonstrations, designed to attract media coverage to individual causes. The demonstrations might be violent anti-abortion presentations or quiet protests against nuclear arms or for a more enlightened immigration policy or hostile pro-feminist protests against the male domination of the priesthood. However, most Catholics do not engage in such demonstrations at all, and, although they may pay attention to, support, or be influenced by them, they are principally involved in their own lives, families, and occupations.

What, in fact, are American Catholics like? According to recent research, some of which we will explore in this chapter, Catholics accept the ideals preached by the church but feel that they can dissent from official opinions when these do not match their own experience or the judgments of their own consciences. What do those who have systematically examined such Catholics tell us about them?

On the extreme, "unchurched" Catholics, defined by James Castelli as those who belong to no parish and have not attended a service in six months, do not feel cut off from the church. The Catholic Church is, in short, a remarkable, family-like phenomenon, not easily summarized in headlines or research reports. It possesses a loyal, loving, and independent constituency who perceive their being Catholics as a deep identity that cannot easily be taken away even by those church leaders who claim to have the authority to do so.

The American Catholic Church, from a review of many current surveys, resembles Siamese twins who are distinct individuals despite the profound sharing of membrane, blood, and genetic inheritance. Yet the comparison fails because Culture Two Catholics, those who are loyal, loving, and independent, have no wish to be separated from Culture One. They want to live with and in it but not blindly acceptant of its total domination. There is something mysterious, real, human, remarkable, and confounding about this extended family of a church that sticks together, much as a big family does, because of deep, satisfying relationships that enable them to overlook each other's faults, love the patriarch even when they no longer agree with him, wish that things would get better while settling for things as they are. It is not easy to simplify or summarize these two interacting cultures whose existence and spirit have been documented by so much research.

James Castelli and George Gallup, Jr., offer a portrait of Catholic America that is generally optimistic and that supports the notions of a church that embraces two cultures.* Against the "conventional wisdom" that Catholic religious activity is declining, for example,

*The American Catholic People: Their Beliefs, Practices, and Values, Garden City, New York, Doubleday, 1987.

they find that "American Catholics are in the middle of a religious revival," marked by stabilized Mass attendance (53 percent), and increased participation in religious activities, including prayer, involvement in church life, and a big increase in Bible reading.*

Perhaps their most interesting finding is that related to the Second Vatican Council and its definition of the church as a People of God. The researchers suggest that, "if that is the criterion, the Council has been a raving success in the United States," where Catholics are secure in their identity. Supporting the remarkable feeling that American Catholics have toward their faith, they note that "Neither criticisms nor disagreements have changed their sense of belonging to the Church; indeed *their sense of ownership of the Church.* "† Furthermore, Castelli and Gallup found that Catholics have more "confidence in the Church than in any other institution," with 85 percent saying that their lifetime experience has been "overall positive." Against this helpful background, which catches the strong feeling Catholics share of the church as a home—"a home," indeed, as the late Albert Cardinal Meyer of Chicago said in a memorable intervention at Vatican II, "for sinners"—we can begin to understand the freedom with which believers disagree with their institutional leaders.

As the researchers observe, Catholics "don't even necessarily want the Church to change all of its teachings with which they disagree; they just want those teachings viewed as ideals which may seem impractical in the real world and from which they may dissent in conscience."‡ These areas of disagreement are, therefore, unlikely to precipitate the departure of these believers from the church to which they feel so strongly attached. Associated with this family feeling is the traditional Catholic sense of sin. Sin, in the Catholic Church, is to be expected, and the contrite can be forgiven readily. These believers are not alarmed by their dissent or by their occasional failings or lapses. It is the pastoral, sacramental church, rather

*Ibid., p. 42.
†Ibid., p. 43. Emphasis added.
‡Ibid.

than the institutional church, in which these Catholics feel so much at home.

That, in conscience, they hold views that differ from those promulgated by the official church becomes somewhat less surprising and less intrinsically contradictory. Thinking for yourself, following your conscience, disagreeing even with the pope: these are perhaps unique freedoms enjoyed by devout American Catholics. They are not, however, the bitter sentiments of people who hate the church or wish to leave it. Church leaders might well ponder this immense good will and loyalty before they interpret these disagreements as some form of deadly and destructive assault on their authority.

A number of research endeavors, including polls conducted for the *National Catholic Reporter,* the *New York Times,* the *New York Times Magazine,* and *Time,* support the general trend of the findings of Castelli and Gallup. On personal moral issues, for example, the latter report that 73 percent of Catholics favor a change in the church's teaching on birth control. The *National Catholic Reporter* found that 66 percent of Catholics felt that they could be in favor of change on this issue and remain good members of the church. The *New York Times* reported 64 percent favoring a change in church policy. So, too, Castelli and Gallup list 69 percent, and the *Times* 66 percent, favoring a change in the church's attitude toward divorce and remarriage for its members. The *National Catholic Reporter* found that 57 percent believed that one could hold this and still be a good Catholic. Even though the great majority of Catholics are against abortion, substantial numbers feel that it is a matter of individual conscience and that circumstances exist in which it could be morally acceptable.

On matters of church policy, similar figures emerge. Many good Catholics believe that women should be ordained to the priesthood and that the discipline of celibacy should be changed. It is in the area of the locus of moral authority, however, that we can observe a major, deeply held conviction of the American Catholic people. As the *National Catholic Reporter* stated, "Catholics are not content with current authority structures in which final decision-making remains solely in the hands of bishops and priests."* This is a succinct statement of the thesis of this book: Culture Two Catholics are not persuaded by the claims to authority of Culture One leaders. They believe that, taking church teachings into account, they should forge their own moral choices.

Thus, on birth control, 62 percent of Catholics believe that the locus of moral authority rests with them while 12 percent believe it rests with church leaders. Even on abortion, about which Catholics have grave reservations, 42 percent hold that the choice must be made by individuals and 29 percent feel that it belongs to church leaders. The question that necessarily arises is whether these views merely reflect American liberal sentiment—as some contend, the "Protestantization" of once-dutiful Catholics—or whether these are convictions reached through the Catholic experience of these people in learning about their faith and in accepting the doctrine of the primacy of conscience. Is the institution that, above all others, insisted on personal responsibility for one's actions discovering that it has taught its people very well indeed, and that these opinions are testimony to the success of Catholic education and evangelization?

There is evidence to support the latter viewpoint. The *National Catholic Reporter*† reports that seven out of ten Catholics would almost never consider leaving the church. Forty-eight percent said that it was "the most important" or "among the most important" parts of life. Another 38 percent described it as "quite important." With such results, one may judge that Catholics regard being a Catholic as a good thing; they are strongly involved and identified with their tradition. A picture of an obstinate, destructive group does not emerge from any of these surveys. What does emerge is something roughly equivalent to Culture Two Catholicism. Catholics support Vatican II overwhelmingly. Any turning back on it,

*September 11, 1987, page 1.
†*Ibid.*, p. 8.

according to Castelli and Gallup, would meet with "widespread, if not almost unanimous, resistance among American Catholics."*

One must not ignore the substantial percentage of Catholics, many of them from Culture One, who do not believe that they can dissent and remain good Catholics at the same time. Those who maintain these convictions are obviously deeply committed and responsive to institutional teaching and authority. They are a source of bedrock strength for administrators and others who feel that "obedience is better than sacrifice," and they represent people deeply imbued with an outlook far more traditional than that of Culture Two Catholics. Not all of these people are of an older generation. Indeed, many older Catholics identify with the second culture. Catholics who choose to accept the church's teaching authority in a deeply traditional way want the institution to flourish; they allow us to understand and appreciate the character of Culture One. Such Catholics support traditional schools, colleges, and newspapers; they are prominent, visible Catholics, who continue to exert influence on church policies. They may, as with dedicated members of such organizations as Opus Dei or Catholics United for the Faith, exercise far more influence on bureaucratic policies and on Roman opinion than Culture Two Catholics who have moved away from the structure.

Other data suggest that many Catholics who might be considered at least adjunct members of Culture Two confine their religious activity to the opportunities inside their own parishes. The ongoing pastoral research project at the University of Notre Dame found large numbers of educated adult Catholics the scope of whose faith convictions remained within that provided by their pastor and his programs. This suggests the continuing effectiveness and resiliency of the parish as a source of identity and opportunity for the practical expression of faith. Some commentators suggested that the lack of broader civic or political involvement was somehow a shortcoming

*Ibid., p. 58.

and that efforts were needed to increase these people's participation in such efforts. A final judgment on this may await further study and analysis. Meanwhile, other expert observers confirm the existence of a second culture of Catholicism and the directions of its growth as well as the problems it faces.

Dr. William McCready, Associate Director of the Public Opinion Laboratory and Associate Professor in the Department of Sociology at Northern Illinois University, has researched the cultures of American Catholicism for several years. Reflecting on his work and his own experience in a phone interview with me, he observed: "For lay Catholics, who are very different from the clergy and religious who are contained by the institutional church and must come to grips with it in their own way, a large number is moving away from caring about the institution at all. They are not concerned about the internal happenings in that culture but they are concerned about religion in their own lives. Most of them feel that their parishes are not dealing with their interest in religion in general, and their spiritual growth and sustenance in particular. If a parish *is* successful in dealing with these matters, that parish is regarded as successful.

"That leads these Catholics to a feeling of intense localization about the church. They do not have much sense of a national or international church. Young people—those from their teens into their thirties—can divorce social action from religiosity. They think that the church should be involved in social action but they don't identify social action as religious in itself. What the younger Catholics are looking for is a more spiritual response from the church, and they want that at an individual level. The parish is set up to respond more to the community than to the individual. But the spiritual need is experienced at the latter level.

"The younger clergy seem torn between their motivation to minister to the spiritual needs of people and their desire to manage. The church has been training the clergy to deal with administrative issues and they are like a group of frustrated MBAs. The reason is that the only reward system surviving in the institution is administrative in nature. All the other symbols, even the small ones such as making priests monsignors, have been eliminated. And there's a great loss there, for these men are seeking administrative recognition and the people need spiritual response.

"What is really at risk is a continuing sense of Catholic identity. For the current population of Catholic adults, there is a tendency for their identity with institutions, including Catholicism, to hang on through much change. But the question is: Will this carry into the future? Two of the great supports of Catholic identity have been rocked. The first is Catholic schools, which are fewer in number, and serve fewer Catholics. The second is the dramatic increase between 1960 and 1985 of mixed marriages. Religious socialization is very different in a mixed marriage than it is in a marriage between two Catholics. That is a problem that nobody in the institution wants to tackle but it has, as the Orthodox Jewish community has found, profound implications for a continuing identity. It is possible that in the next century Catholics will be ten percent rather than a quarter of the population.

"The main problem, I believe, for institutional continuity lies elsewhere. An institution like the Catholic Church that lays claim to moral leadership and at the same time rules out the full participation of women is bound to fail. There is no way that the institution is defensible on the way it deals with women. And, as it tries to maintain itself in exercises of damage control on other issues, such as covering up cases of pedophilia among priests, the institution weakens itself even more. In my judgment, well over half of American Catholics—perhaps in the range of sixty to sixty-five percent—are moving away from the institution."

Nonetheless, Catholics remain strongly identified at this time with their church, especially in terms of its sacramental nature and presence in their lives. In a trenchant essay on "Why Catholics Stay in the Church," Andrew Greeley offers a thesis that explains the existence and the enduring enthusiasm of Culture Two Catholics for a faith that they do not identify with the authoritarian claims of the institutional church.* He writes that "the decision to remain Catholic (or to reidentify as Catholic) does not mean that the laity continue to be Catholic on the terms the institutional church requires. . . . Catholics therefore stay. They stay on their own terms, but they stay. Moreover, anyone who associates with Catholic laity . . . knows that the anguish of the media or the troubled faith of the Vatican and the hierarchy simply do not exist for most of the laity."

Father Greeley sees a loyalty compounded of three elements as the force that keeps Catholics in the church. They find identity in the Catholic heritage, they find community in the Catholic parish, and, most significant of all, the "sacramentality of Catholicism has tremendous appeal for the imaginative dimension of personality."† I believe he is exactly correct in saying that "the Eucharist holds together all three components."

Culture One, therefore, is intensely loyal, conscientious, religious, and bound to the church by the sacramental tradition that speaks with convincing authority to its imagination. Its dynamism is a source of organic growth that will affect the institution whether the institution consciously chooses to be affected or not. Despite its many problems, the American Catholic Church seems to be alive, interested, reasonably content, and peaceful of conscience. That is not a bad definition of a successful church.

*America, August 1–8, 1987, p. 54.
†Ibid., pp. 57, 70.

6

Side by Side

Substance and Accidents
in the Two Cultures

. . . so too we, though many, are one body in Christ and individually members of one another . . .
—Romans 12:5

One of you will say, "I belong to Paul," another "I belong to Apollos". . . . Has Christ then been divided into parts?
—I Corinthians 1:12–13

Allowing for a certain amount of interpretation and a mixture of compatibility and tension, what do these Catholic cultures look like in real life, who inhabits them, and how do they differ from one another?

It is helpful to begin with Pope John Paul II, for, while he symbolizes Culture One as its institutional leader, he is no stranger to Culture Two. Intensely conscious of the nearly impossible task of binding a diverse billion-member congregation together through his own institutional office and person, he has also demonstrated his philosopher's interest in the world's own problems, his dramatist's awareness of human nature, and his actor's presence on the public stage. John Paul is, however, first and foremost the leader of the institution, and its survival and welfare, as well as the preservation of papal teaching authority, are constantly on his mind. Howsoever one may judge his tactics, his purpose in consolidating the institutional church as consciously unified and loyal to him is as understandable as it is undisguised.

Pope John Paul's citizenship in Culture Two cannot, if only because of the glare of public attention, be easily distinguished from his role as pontiff. Still, if one looks and listens closely, one senses a shrewd mover, aware of intermingled secular and religious tradition, who does not hesitate to act in a purely political manner. The irony of his direct intervention in Polish politics has been noted by those who observe that this same pope has rigorously ruled the priests of the world out of active politics. They belong, he implies, within the institution, but he moves, slightly bent as if weighed down with his own national history, into the fray of Polish civil life without hesitation.

On his pilgrimages to his native land, the pope harnesses the energy of the people through the institutional church. The cultures mesh together in this much aggrieved land and the pope keeps his hands on the controls. To the world at large, Polish Catholicism and the Polish impulse to freedom are almost indistinguishable. What is obscured underneath the institutional claims to vitality—to plenty of church buildings and a rich harvest of vocations—is the existence of any other consciousness of what it means to be Catholic.

The beloved pope so dominates the scene that truths about everyday Polish Catholic life are seldom examined. They exist, nonetheless, and insiders readily admit that institutional control of everyday life is not as pervasive as it seems on the surface. There is still a higher ratio of priests to people in the United States, for example, and, in the mid-seventies, the proportion of abortions was higher in this Catholic country than it was in the United States. A second culture does indeed exist even in the Poland that the pope holds up as a model of what a nation that keeps its faith should be.

Pope John Paul II, extraordinary as a man and a world figure, is committed to institutional ends by his very office. He is the first citizen of Culture One and he enters Culture Two on his own terms. He differs from Pope John XXIII, who was able to speak easily and directly to the world beyond the institution, non-Catholics included. He influenced the institution profoundly, gaining leverage over it by pursuing broader goals. In fact, as theologian Gabriel Daly puts it, John XXIII colluded "with a council in its challenge to the power of his own bureaucracy." John XXIII placed the church at risk as an institution and, despite the trauma of the transitional years, drew it out of its exile and made it once more a subject of history. It is not yet clear whether Pope John Paul II is strengthening the institution by his more deliberate efforts to do so. In some ways, and despite the freedom of movement he allows himself geographically, the present pope's style tends to define the church over against the world, to emphasize its organizational needs even as he proclaims its spiritual teachings. And what of his spiritual teachings? They aim largely at bolstering the institution and its control over the spiritual lives of its people. While he battles for political freedom in Poland, it is unclear that he is committed to spiritual or intellectual freedom in the church at large.

The pope, by virtue of his office, generates a number of enterprises that are uniquely and totally the products of Culture One. These range from papal audiences to papal blessings; the best example, of course, is the papal trip. The 1987 journey to the United States was conceived, planned, and executed through the institutional church, of which the pilgrimage is a prime function and powerful symbol. That American papal pilgrimage, even in retrospect, is extraordinarily relevant to the citizens of Culture One; it lights up the darkened corners of the institutional culture, excites the enthusiasm of its members, enlists their participation, seeks their support for its success in a hundred ways. The objective of any papal visit is, of course, fundamentally institutional: it is aimed at strengthening people's loyalty to the church's authority over their religious and moral lives and to the office of the pope as the symbol of its unity. As the flight of the Wright brothers was related to fabric and wooden struts, so the papal visit is related to the apparatus of the hierarchical church. While there is no need to apologize for the use of such means in the pursuit of structural ends, it is also important to note that Culture Two does not find the papal pilgrimage as necessary, relevant, absorbing, or as vital as Culture One does.

.The question for Culture Two citizens, quite unlike that for Culture One, was not *how shall we receive the pope?* but rather, *how will he speak to us?* Catholics of the second culture remain too involved in their own lives to be carried away by the spectacle of a pope's arrival. That does not suggest indifference as much as absorption in the affairs of their own lives—raising children, working, carrying out civic and political responsibilities, facing crises of an assorted and unlimited variety—through which they understand, undemonstratively and unselfishly, that they express and apply their religious convictions.

Such Catholics feel, in accord with the theology of Vatican II and with no disrespect for the pope, that they are as much the church as he is. They do not, therefore, want, in an experience of the intensely hierarchical mode with which they are all too familiar, to be talked down to. These Catholics accept the papacy as an office of spiritual leadership but not one of stratified royal prerogative. They long, as a matter of fact, for the pope to speak to their experience in a way that reveals his sensitive grasp of what their lives and struggles are like. His authority as a teacher would be enhanced by even simple expressions of such pastoral compassion. When, however, the pope speaks as if from a throne, *ex cathedra,* as the formula goes, in monarchical regalia, expecting Catholics to accept an old ordering of their relationship to the church and to him, he diminishes rather than expands his teaching authority.

Papal visits, then, are largely Culture One affairs. That they dominate the television screen does not mean that they dominate the imaginations of most Catholics. That such visits have lost some of their appeal to the broadcasting industry was evidenced in the fact that only the CBS network hired a full-time priest consultant to assist in covering the 1987 trip. It was not considered worthy of that much analysis by the other networks. Such national journeys represent the institution displaying itself to itself and for itself. Even the crowds, judged even by the trip's sponsors to be disappointing in some places, were gathered and managed by institutional planners. In truth, papal visits belong to a bygone era of spectacles, of world fairs and centenary exhibitions, of nineteenth-century circuses, Teddy Roosevelt's great white fleet sailing majestically into the great harbors of the world to show the flag. Absent evidence that the pope comprehends the profound religious longings and genuine spiritual maturity of great numbers of Culture Two citizens, his visit is far less influential for them than its Culture One planners think it is.

American Catholics in both cultures are serious about their religious obligations. The citizens of each of these cultures can be identified easily in many areas of life. William F. Buckley, Jr., still enamored of the elite Catholicism of *Brideshead Revisited* (he did the concluding comments on the PBS version of the novel) is a proud citizen of Culture One. Father Theodore Hesburgh, former president of Notre Dame University, although in some ways a highly traditional clergyman, has always lived and functioned confidently in Culture Two. Hesburgh's viewpoint and values have always been universal, his interest in and understanding of world problems transcending the perimeters of institutional concerns. The field of government offers many examples of contemporary Catholics who dwell in these separate cultures.

Representative Henry Hyde (R., Illinois) is a Culture One Catholic who proudly advocates the convictions and interests of the church as an institution. He supports its authority and has given his name to the amendment that limits federal funding for abortions, a prime cause of institutional Catholicism. Congressman Hyde's commitments parallel those of the bishops and he does not hesitate to defend, for example, the teaching authority of the church to his fellow Catholics. He nonetheless symbolizes a Catholic figure from that sophisticated generation that succeeded the era in which City Hall, the Police Department, and the Catholic Church were hopelessly intermingled entities in many American cities. In that period numerous families boasted at least one son in each of these organizations. Henry Hyde is a transformed, polished inheritor of that same tradition and makes no apologies for representing it vigorously. It also makes political sense to him, since he represents a heavily Catholic area of Illinois. Still Hyde sees himself as a defender of the faith. He spoke, for example, at Notre Dame University in the fall of 1984 to rebut the speech given a few weeks previously by Culture Two member Democratic Governor Mario Cuomo of New York, on the obligation of a Catholic civic official to support the laws of the land even if, in certain circumstances, it clashed with his Catholic principles. Catholics might try to change the law, according to Cuomo, by every moral argument and persuasion, but they should not flout the law fashioned in a society in which honest disagreements existed between people of good faith.

Cuomo is a prominent embodiment of Culture Two. Educated in the first culture, he has come, as a serious student of Vatican II theology, to live and reflect on his faith in the second culture. Cuomo has not been intimately associated with institutional Catholicism and has not built his career on such an association. His positions have, in fact, brought him criticism at times from Culture One leaders. He obviously understands as well as Henry Hyde what is to his political advantage, but he openly professes his faith and does not hesitate to discuss its theology as he contemplates the serious moral questions that confront a public official in a pluralistic society. He is far more like the average Catholic of his generation than John F. Kennedy was of his. Kennedy was a patrician, born to wealth and Harvard educated, a Catholic still fighting prejudice, who, in a famous speech before Baptist ministers shortly before his election, had to disclaim Vatican influence to prove that he was a loyal American. Whatever his personal outlook, Kennedy lived in an era in which Culture One was dominant in American life. Nineteen sixty, the year he was elected, was a high-water mark for the institutional culture of American Catholicism. It was the summit of achievement in the construction of churches, schools, and seminaries; the summit whose shadows fell directly onto a downward slope.

Cuomo, the son of immigrants, a St. John's University graduate, belongs to that generation of Catholics that has developed a consciousness of citizenship in the second culture. Cuomo thinks for himself but not randomly, for he reflects as a sophisticated Catholic on his own Catholic tradition and in accord with the principles of its theology. He does not ask church officials what he should say, and in his occasional skirmishes with members of the hierarchy apparently feels their equal in applying his faith in his life and work. In fact, he is the equal of most priests and bishops in theological understanding precisely because of his university-level Catholic education and his continuing interest in matters of the faith. He looms, irrespective of how one judges his political views, as a classic Culture Two Catholic.

Other Voices, Other Rooms

To shift to a very different field that anticipates one of our later concerns, the contemporary appraisal of sanctity also provides us with illustrations of cultural differences within American Catholicism. Declaring somebody a saint is so closely associated in our imaginations with the institutional church that we may be dulled to the incongruity of this situation. To think that a massive bureaucracy, no matter what its intentions, should, with all its clanking machinery, be the arbiter of the goodness of individual lives is, if we look freshly at it, startling. An excellent case can be made for never allowing bureaucrats to make statements about the spiritual life. It is outside their range.

We may observe in this matter elaborate bureaucratic procedures involved in pursuing the cause of an aspiring saint. We discover an enormous concern for purity and freedom from the taint of the flesh and from the inevitable decompositional fate of more earthbound mortals, indeed, for evidence of a body that defies the decay of death. This model of sanctity is drawn on finely lined paper that matches the minutely graded levels of the hierarchical steps to the rarefied atmosphere of the holy. This emphasizes the estrangement of the natural from the supernatural, of earth from heaven, producing the fundamental out-of-jointness that, as we shall see, is the root of much confusion about the nature and practice of religion and spirituality.

In this version of sanctity, the aspirant breaks ties with earth, riding the slowly ascending rocket of holiness, jettisoning human attachments and needs, rising above the elements that constitute the ordinary experience of most mortals. This Cartesian achievement of separating soul from body at the latter's expense was attested to by the identifiable signs that survived the saint's life, an incorruptible body being one of the expected indications.

The essence of such a notion of sanctity lay in perceiving nature as an enemy to be conquered, a notion not very different from that which justified industrial entrepreneurs in stripping forests and poisoning rivers in order to feed commerce and nourish fortunes. The saints were thought to have turned successfully away from the simple experiences that constitute the lives of ordinary people. It is parenthetically significant to note that this hierarchical model of sanctity has for centuries been totally under the control of male ecclesiastical administrators. In short, the Roman congregation that oversees the making of saints has done so, as we will discuss at greater length later, by a thoroughly masculine supervision of the parameters of sanctity. This congregation is better observed in its true nature as a breeder of other bureaucracies, for one comes elaborately into being for each individual whose cause for sanctity is introduced. This includes setting up offices, soliciting funds, appointing officials with titles that ring with institutional connotations, such as postulator and vice-postulator of the hopeful cause. They eventually deal with the ultimate Roman bureaucrat, the devil's advocate, the keeper of doubts and questions about the proposed saint's life and works.

That holy lives should be ground so fine in bureaucratic mills offends good sense while it illustrates the enormous control the institutional church exercises over matters that are essentially noninstitutional. It suggests the dense texture of Culture One. Culture Two, harking back to the habits of early Christian communities, spontaneously recognizes holy people, intuitively calling them *good,* without any need for organizational validation of their judgment. Sanctity by acclamation is the judgment of lively believers, the holy wisdom of the community, the common sense of genuine spirituality that has not been divorced from life. Thus St. Francis of Assisi has a continuing broad appeal that cuts across faiths and cultures, not because he was officially canonized, but because of the pure nature of the life he led. Francis's authority comes from within himself, not from the institution. Indeed, at times the Franciscan ideal, with its spirit of generous freedom, has been perceived as a threat to the institutional interests of the church.

In our day, that popular acclamation of goodness has obviously gone to Pope John XXIII. His official cause of canonization, however, has been delayed for institutional political reasons. Powerful ecclesiastical figures, employing a favorite phrase of the bureaucracy, consider it "inopportune" for the church to put its seal on a judgment about his goodness long ago made by the Christian people. Ironically, Pope Pius X, who condemned "Modernism" so vigorously in the first decade of the century and so, as we will presently discuss, brought on the repression of the Catholic intellectual life, was declared a saint less than fifty years later. A man, it would seem, much more acceptable to the bureaucrats.

In the summer of 1987 in Detroit, according to the ghoulish procedures of Roman congregations, the body of a priest, Father Solanus Casey, already recognized as good during his lifetime, was exhumed, inspected, and reburied in a coffin bearing the waxen seal of the archbishop, Edmund Szoka. The medieval character of these proceedings was footnoted by a Monsignor Allen who witnessed them. The remains, he said, were "an intact body—however, not perfectly so." This good priest, who counseled people for decades and ran a soup kitchen during the Depression, whose cause was officially introduced shortly after his death in 1957, had been subjected to Culture One profanation. Culture Two Catholics have no taste for such gruesomeness, or for measures of holiness that depend even in part on a dead body's preservation, ambiguous evidence, at best, of virtue. Such notions, which rob holiness of its everyday possibilities, do not speak to the problem of leading a good life in our time. They reflect antique institutional preoccupations, hierarchical measures of holiness, and a bureaucratic management of sanctity that is strongly, if unconsciously, motivated by the need to control people even after death. One must wonder at the multiplication of beatifications and canonizations that have occurred in the pontificate of John Paul II. They are fragments from an old, now largely incomprehensible, institutional language spoken largely inside Culture One Catholicism.

Clinging to the first culture like information to a microchip are dozens of devotional styles, many of which gave great comfort to believers, and some of which, as we shall see later, were more complex than they at first appear. That there has been a shift in Catholic devotional habits is undeniable. The Mass has emerged in Culture Two as the central sacramental mystery that, despite efforts to make it more rational by translating it into the vernacular, speaks to the deepest levels of human personality in a compelling manner. One may contrast this with the exercises and devotions that, in the judgment of many observers, tended to obscure the Mass in the heyday of Culture One. The reemergence of the Eucharist as the inexhaustible mystery that speaks in its own way and from its own depths to the depths of those in attendance is an extraordinary triumph for religion in general and for Vatican II's theology in particular.

Still, the advertising pages of most Catholic papers (themselves the products of institutional life) are filled with evidence of the lingering vigor of Culture One. On one page of *Catholic Twin Circle* in the month before the 1987 American papal visit, one could find advertisements for a "beautifully sculptured plaque of Pope John Paul II, in bronze gold relief on a rich walnut-like finish, includes commemorative brass plate . . . $29.95 plus $2.50 to cover shipping. Or use your MasterCard or Visa. ACT NOW AS QUANTITIES ARE LIMITED." Next to it was an ad for the Marian Year Papal Coin. "Order now and enjoy special pre-minting price . . . $20.00 each."

Of such was the kingdom of God. These are not souvenirs that speak very loudly to Culture Two Catholics.

America's two Catholic cultures may also be distinguished in terms of the voices to which they listen. For decades, Culture One offered a definition of itself through its tight control over the transmission of intellectual theory, popular thought, political philosophy, general information, education, entertainment, and art to the Catholic populace. Through effective instrumentations that included the Index of Forbidden Books, the Legion of Decency, the constant reiteration of the dangers of Communism, non-Catholic colleges, and much modern art, church leaders kept the circle of so-called "worldly" stimulation closed. An acceptable Catholic novel, for example, was generally a pious work that supported and encouraged Catholic ideals and practices and justified the institution and its control over the lives of its adherents. In such works, the good were rewarded, the erring, terribly punished. Artists, in any medium, who challenged the institution's tame limits of acceptability were often roundly condemned. Thinking at all was considered dangerous and, for many Catholics in the fifties, Bishop Fulton J. Sheen summed up the church's intellectual life on his enormously popular telecasts, in which he gave a half-hour lecture every week on an aspect of Catholic doctrine. These programs (he beat comedian Milton Berle in his time slot) were virtually the only experience large numbers of Catholics had of any bishop's treating a scholarly subject at all. And these programs were apologetic in the classical sense, for they were skilled arguments for traditional church teaching or against such threats as Communism. They represented the wisdom of a seemingly ageless creed confronting the modern world. The questions raised were rhetorical rather than motivated by intellectual curiosity. The programs made Catholics feel better about themselves the way a John Wayne movie made Americans feel better about themselves.

Until Vatican II, the basic set of the institutional church in America was defensive. This was perhaps essential to its establishment and nurturance in a republic that arose out of a revolution against royal domination and was innately suspicious of Catholics loyal to what

Protestant America perceived as a threatening foreign power. Catholic bishops and priests fought vigorously, often heroically, for the rights of their immigrant flocks; the church felt keenly its obligation to protect its people from the dangers of the surrounding, potentially infective, American Protestant culture. Thus it rigidly guarded its parishoners' civil rights and their moral lives, staking out picket lines beyond which Catholics could not venture except at risk to their souls. Catholics were trained first to understand their faith in an unsophisticated way, then to defend it.

Loyal Catholics were not to be too curious about the world's interpretation of things, or about questions or issues that seemed likely to subvert their faith. Thus, the church's long suspicion and oversimplified condemnation of the theories of thinkers such as Charles Darwin and Sigmund Freud, its muscular readiness to restrict the indiscriminate reading of books, the viewing of movies, or attendance at any college where a philosophical system other than Thomism was presented. As late as 1957, the Vatican congregation on education said that coeducation could never be defended "in principle," although it might be permitted for pragmatic reasons. It is small wonder that artists who explored themes that seemed even slightly to challenge the institution or its view of itself—to explore the tortured depths of a certain strain of Irish family life as Eugene O'Neill and James T. Farrell did—were hardly welcome or comfortable within its boundaries.

While one may rightly appreciate many of these paternalistic actions as fine for their time and place, one would hardly be disobedient to acknowledge that they now seem dated and that their power to speak to the experience of well-educated Catholic people is limited if not altogether absent. Culture Two believers find their intellectual, religious, and artistic stimulation well beyond the tightly guarded borders of this quaint Catholic enclave, in the broader resources in the contemporary world. They no longer need specifically "Catholic" books or films; such Catholics hear and sense the religious dimension in any honest work of art; they are much more at home in the world in general than their parents were permitted to be. This represents an exodus, true as that by which the Jewish people left Egypt, out of the restricted and carefully supervised environment of a previous era of Catholicism, a passage out of a time when everything was made simple into an understanding of how extraordinarily complicated everything of value really is.

The following table is suggestive of the membership in the two cultures of Catholicism.

CULTURE ONE	CULTURE TWO
John Paul II	John Paul II
Deacons	Lay ministers
The Wanderer	*National Catholic Reporter*
Archbishop Edmund Szoka	John Cardinal Dearden
Evelyn Waugh	John Gregory Dunne
Joseph Cardinal Bernardin	Joseph Cardinal Bernardin
Bernard Cardinal Law	Archbishop Rembert Weakland
Vocation drives	Lay ministry
Phyllis Schlafly	Geraldine Ferraro
Body parts	The whole person
Catholic United for the Faith	National Conference of Catholic Bishops (in session)
Michael Novak	Daniel Callahan (despite his protests)
Charismatics	Everyone else
University of Notre Dame	University of Notre Dame
Any papal knight	Any Catholic artist
European traditions	Democratic traditions
Frank Capra	Francis Ford Coppola
William F. Buckley, Jr.	Jimmy Breslin
Joseph Cardinal Ratzinger	David Tracy
Mother Teresa	Mother Teresa
Papal visits	Family gatherings
The author	The author

You get the idea.

7

Where the Road Divides

The Two Cultures:
The Roots of Difference

*Wisdom is the principal thing; therefore get wisdom: and with
all thy getting get understanding. . . .*
—Proverbs 4:7

*Two roads diverged in a wood, and I—
I took the one less traveled by,
And that has made all the difference.*
—Robert Frost, "The Road Not Taken"

*The Miracles of the Church seem to me to rest not so much upon
the faces or voices or healing power coming suddenly near to us
from afar off, but upon our perceptions being made finer, so that
for a moment our eyes can see and our ears can hear what is
there about us always.*
—Willa Cather, *Death Comes for the Archbishop*

As noted, the most significant link between Culture Two Catholics
and their church is sacramental. The genius of the sacramental first
nature of the church (institutionalization is only second nature) is
that, through the potent, living vocabulary of symbols, it points to,
preserves, and nourishes the inner lives of God's people. Bureau-

crats may obsessively supervise the outer lives of Catholics, and even the exterior notes and conditions of the administration of the sacraments themselves. It was no accident that, during the great building era of American Catholicism, which came to an end roughly at the time of Vatican II, priests trained in canon law taught the moral theology courses in almost all major seminaries. "Keep the law," a mildly ironic saying of the period went, "and the law will keep you."

But the good life, much less the holy life, is not, as ordinary people understand, a function merely of obsessive lawkeeping. That approach, as we have noted, was condemned by Jesus as a crippled and hypocritical understanding of the nature of religion. The sacramental church grasps the spiritual reality beneath the everyday world of appearances; it senses intuitively where the mystery of existence lies and celebrates and illuminates those moments without exhausting or, for that matter, explaining them fully. The sacraments hallow those intersections of existence in which we feel, even as the prophets did, the breath of the spirit on our necks and in our hearts. The language of the sacraments is, therefore, not legal but metaphorical. Culture One officials, more in the tradition of Enlightenment rationalists than Christian mystics, have attempted to establish and control the logic of religion and of the sacraments, to render them as linear, orderly, supervisable experiences when, as common people understand, they are nothing of the kind.

Although this failure or muting of instincts can be seen in many programs and policies of the official church, its principal symptom is a loss of fluency in the language of spirituality. This may be seen in the adaptation of shallow contemporary psychological jargon, which gives only a faint echo of sacramental reality. It is footnoted by the admission of many American bishops in research interviews of their difficulties with the spiritual side of their calling, especially with prayer. They feel much more comfortable with administrative work. Similarly, one of the recent vogues in workshops for priests and religious has been the intensive journal keeping recommended by psychologist Ira Progoff; he urges them to "get a new Now . . . the Open Moment of our life." This is paralleled by the widespread use in parishes of the Myers-Briggs personality inventory as a proposed source of the self-knowledge that has been a traditional goal of spiritual growth. Such superficial and questionable techniques clutter the vacuum that develops in any institution that has lost touch with the true language of the soul.

Such approaches exemplify the division of heaven from earth, the separation of eternity from time, of soul from body, sacred from secular, and word from sacrament characteristic of a heavily organizational church. A classic illustration occurred near the end of 1987 when Rome's Sacred Congregation for Divine Worship, revealing no saving sense of irony, solemnly forbade in Catholic churches any concerts of music that was not religious. In the same decree they demanded that groups that do perform in churches "must sign an agreement beforehand to clean up after themselves." This bureaucratic triumph, with its sigh of middle-age frustration with youth's lack of tidiness, repeated the plaguing artificial distinction between religious and nonreligious artistic works, underscoring the persistence of the divided model of the person—that slash between heaven and earth—as still functional inside Culture One.

The official church's commitment of its authority to a literalist interpretation of religious experience has caused it to concretize metaphor, mistaking denotation for connotation, and, as Joseph Campbell puts it, "the messenger for the message, overloading the carrier, consequently, with sentimentalized significance and throwing both life and thought thereby out of balance."* In other words, the very teachers who should be most sensitive and responsive to the sacraments as the movable feasts at which we gather to glimpse the transcendence of experience have tried to tie them down in time and location, to control rather than reverence them.

Mystery roils like foggy mist in the gaps and chasms of existence; it is the stuff, the essence of religious experience. The nature of faith is radically altered if ambivalence is extracted from it. That happens

*The Inner Reaches of Outer Space, New York, Alfred Van Der Marck Editions, 1986, p. 58.

when the metaphors of the spiritual life are translated as literal incidents in religion conceived of as a historic pageant. And Culture One leaders have tended to treat the symbolic language of faith in this manner during the twentieth century, thereby associating their authority as religious teachers with petrified and dehydrated versions of what are really rich and nourishing religious experiences. Such strategies not only damage their authority in the long run but they forge faith into brittle orthodoxies that easily become sources of factional strife. As Campbell writes:

> In the popular nightmare of history, where local mythic images are interpreted, not as metaphors, but as facts, there have been ferocious wars waged between the parties of such contrary manners of metaphoric representation. The Bible abounds in examples. And today, in the formerly charming little city of Beirut, the contending zealots of three differing inflections even of the same idea of a single paternal "God" are unloading bombs on each other.*

How did these differing approaches—the one literal and legal, the other metaphorical and sacramental—come to be the sources of energy for the two cultures of American Catholicism?

This may be traced, I believe, to that moment at the very beginning of the twentieth century when Catholic scholars and bishops stood together, in Robert Frost's metaphor, at the fork of two roads that "diverged in a wood." The scripture scholars and theologians, enthusiastic about the scholarly rediscovery of the mytho-poetic nature of the Bible and the associated learning of the "new criticism," foresaw the opening of an exciting era in which the ancient spiritual energies of the sacred books could be tapped freshly. Of the divided paths, they wanted to take "the one less travelled by." But the bishops, responding to enormous institutional pressure, insisted that the church move along the traditional way, rejecting metaphor as

*Ibid.

they embraced literalism in the interpretation of the scriptures. As the poet concluded, "that has made all the difference."

A tragic and far-reaching event occurred in American Catholicism in the first decade of the century as a bright, vigorous flame of intellectual advance was snuffed out by the thoroughly devastating reaction of Pope Pius X to a movement termed "Modernism." In the United States, the center of the revival of learning was St. Joseph's Seminary, the training ground for priests of the archdiocese of New York located just beyond the city line at Dunwoodie in Westchester County. There, under the Reverend James Driscoll, himself a Biblical scholar and an Orientalist, a program of priestly education that would still seem remarkable at the end of the century was instituted. Driscoll believed that priests should be educated as well as, and in relationship to, other professional persons. The seminary curriculum and guest lecturers reflected a grasp of the new scholarship of the Bible and an enormous intellectual curiosity about cultural and scientific subjects. Driscoll, along with the Father Patrick Duffy who would later become famous as chaplain of the "Fighting Sixty-ninth" regiment in World War One, established the first scholarly Catholic theological journal in the country, *The New York Review*. Another would not be launched for almost forty years.

This remarkable rector, who understood that the metaphorical language of the scriptures bore the depth of their spiritual and theological significance, arranged with Nicholas Murray Butler, then president of Columbia University, for the seminarians to take courses there and also established an exchange program with the Union Theological Seminary. The prospect of an American Catholic Church that was intellectually sophisticated as well as muscularly determined existed, electrically, hopefully, and briefly. Then, as historian Michael V. Gannon writes in his classic treatment of the matter:

The lightning struck finally in 1907. On July 3 of that year, the Holy Office issued a syllabus, *Lamentabili sane exitu*, listing sixty-five heretical propositions. . . . And on September 8, Pius

X issued an encyclical, *Pascendi Dominici gregis,* condemning the errors of what the pontiff called "modernism." . . . Implied in the encyclical's description . . . were such diverse tools or directions of thought as historical criticism, literary exegesis separate from dogma, naturalistic evolutionary philosophy . . . all systems of thought by whatever name which expounded an evolutionary theory of religion, or suggested that the Church had reshaped eternal truths in every period of history according to its understanding, or otherwise threatened the validity and stability of dogma. . . . [The] typical modernist was a manifold personality: he was a philosopher, a believer, a theologian, an historian, a critic, an apologist, and a reformer. His heresy was . . . that he had used his knowledge "to subvert the Kingdom of Christ," principally by his suggestion that the essence of Christianity lay not in intellectual propositions nor in creeds, but in the very processes of life.*

The condemnation of the budding intellectual renaissance was implemented by disciplinary moves that included the ultimate closing of the *Review* and the replacement of the scholarly rector with the chaplain of the New York Police Department, a good man who had proved his bravery as priest on the battleship *Maine* when it went down off Cuba in 1898 but who lacked any scholarly credentials. An era of military-like control and discipline began. The faculty was broken up and Driscoll, a great, tragically lost figure in American Catholic history, became a pastor and never published again. Many of the records of his years at Dunwoodie have disappeared from the archives, along with most traces of his correspondence. That Father Duffy came to be remembered as a war hero with a statue in the heart of clamorous New York city, instead of as a pioneering theologian, poignantly and ironically symbolizes the preferred emphasis of the then powerfully ascendant Culture One.

The silence imposed on these priests was paralleled across the

*"Before And after Modernism: The Intellectual Isolation of The American Priest" in *The Catholic Priest in the United States,* Collegeville, Minn., St. John's University Press, 1971, pp. 335, 336.

country by moves that turned seminaries into highly controlled institutions, in which association with the general intellectual life of the broader American culture was effectively forbidden. The road taken did indeed make all the difference, for, in revisiting this repressive episode one stands at the fork in the woods, one path of which led to a highly successful, indeed somewhat glorious if heavily institutionalized Culture One Catholicism. The other led, after long years of an achingly slow recovery of the intellectual possibilities of Catholicism, to the development of Culture Two, a deinstitutionalized, sacramental gathering of the spiritual descendants of Driscoll and Duffy. For Culture Two seeks the religious treasures that Culture One, just before the imperial age collapsed forever, refused to examine before it put them under lock and key in the deepest vaults of its castellated self.

Culture Two Catholics have suffered from the sacramental deprivation that flowed from this extraordinary rejection of the ambiguity and complexity of religion as a mysterious, organic reality. As the century draws toward its end, many Culture One hardliners, such as the editors of the St. Paul–based *Wanderer* newspaper, defend Pius X's condemnation of Modernism and identify it as the abiding, infectious heresy of the day. In a recent denunciation, Ann Roche Muggeridge blames Modernists for what she perceives as the destruction of traditional Catholicism, averring that "a more contradictory and exasperating religious position is difficult to imagine."* But genuine Culture Two Catholics are not seeking to overturn or debunk traditional religion, although these charges continue to be made. They are rather continuing the pilgrimage begun by men such as Driscoll and Duffy; they are looking for precisely what the first culture chooses, out of misunderstanding or fear that historical literalism will be lost, not to allow them to experience of the Christian spiritual and mystical tradition.

The anxiety inside Culture One, as illustrated by Mrs. Mug-

The Desolate City: Revolution in the Catholic Church, San Francisco, Harper & Row, 1986, p. 28.

geridge and many others, is that an approach to the principal incidents of the Judeo-Christian religious tradition that questions their historical accuracy also dooms them as supportive illustrations of God's intervention in time and His will for our salvation. It is as if, on a global scale, Culture Two wants to play the Clarence Darrow role while placing Culture One in the dock as William Jennings Bryan. By the end of the cross-examination, historical Biblical religion would be a shambles, and people would be left with nothing in which to believe. As Mrs. Muggeridge puts it,

> The problem of how best to reconcile the findings of history and science with faith as handed down through the ages faces the Church in this as in every age. . . . No common ground in which to anchor a new synthesis exists between scholars who deny the rational basis of Christian dogma and the Church, which puts itself on record for modern times as continuing "firmly and with absolute constancy to hold that the four gospels . . . whose historical character the Church unhesitatingly asserts, faithfully hand on what Jesus Christ, while living among men, really did and taught for their eternal salvation until the day He was taken up into Heaven"—*Dei Verbum,* 19.*

The roots of the two discernible cultures can be traced back to this split, which found the official church remaining on what it believed to be the main, secure road of literal Biblical understanding. Culture Two Catholics, revived intellectually, find themselves on a different but familiar road that pursues, as they understand it, not the barren de-mythologization of Catholic teaching but the rediscovery of its sacramental essence and spiritual meaning. While critics such as Mrs. Muggeridge suggest that those we call Culture Two Catholics are intent on stripping away historical Christianity to leave a desolated place, contemporary Catholics do not see this as their objective at all. Instead, they want to grasp the language in which the deepest truths

Ibid., p. 32.

about our personalities have been spoken, and to recapture the sacramental richness that is obscured when everything is interpreted in a concrete and literalist manner. They do not feel, for example, that in exploring the spiritual meaning of the story of creation they are destroying belief but are rather coming to understand better the religious character and application of Genesis as they never could if the occurrence were treated solely as an individual, totally linear historical account.

The reading of essentially symbolic material as if it were hard, factual historical data, such as the Biblical account of the creation of the world and the fall of an actual pair of first parents, insisted upon rigorously as recently as 1950 by Pope Pius XII in his encyclical *Humani Generis,* slighted the spiritual significance of these metaphors. Metaphors, it must be remembered are not lies but extraordinarily supple vessels of truth. The "fall," for example, is to be read as a *religious* rather than a historical account, as a spiritual message about our interior lives. It is, in fact, as Campbell writes, "a variant of the universally known *Separation of Heaven and Earth,* where the consciousness of an intelligible 'Presence' informing all the transformations of the temporal shapes of the world is represented as having been in some way, at some moment, lost, with the mind and spirit of mankind then trapped in phenomenality alone."* The function of religion is to repair this shattered connection (*religion* comes, indeed, from *re-ligare,* to rejoin), so that all might grasp that the "Kingdom of God," as Jesus said, "is within you," to summon up, in other words, a sacramental universe as a unity lighted from within by wonder and meaning.

Such readings of scripture as essentially metaphoric opens them to us and hardly robs us of spirituality. Metaphor, from the words for *to make a journey across boundaries,* is the natural language of the internal life, the imagination, the spirit, the soul. It refers to that interior world, that vast scape as limitless as outer space, that corresponds to eternity even as the body corresponds to time. Yet the

*Campbell, p. 61.

option for the literal has led Catholicism back to that same fork in the road from which this estrangement began. The roots of the seemingly opposed cultures may be traced to that place where the road split in the first decade of the century. What the institutional church gained in strongly asserting its command over the consciences and behaviors of its clergy and its people it has gradually lost as the latter have reawakened to their own spiritual longing for a faith that is truly sacramental and therefore revelatory of the transcendent spiritual realities of existence.

The central question, as we will now observe, becomes, as it has been throughout the century for all great institutions, that of authority. What kind of authority is emphasized in Culture One? Is it generative and healthy, or controlling and fearful of loss? Has the institution, through its strong commitment to a concrete, historically based faith, lost its feeling for the spiritual mystical authority that distinguished Jesus when he rose to speak in the temple? Are the members of Culture Two merely seeking to escape the restrictions of authority so that they can believe anything they please? Or are they seeking, deeply and sincerely, for the inner seams of faith, for the deep spiritual meanings that are still to be found in every solid tradition of the church?

PART TWO

THE SEARCH
FOR
SPIRITUAL AUTHORITY

8

Moonstruck

The Collapse of Hierarchical Cultures

Canst thou bind the sweet influences of Pleiades, or loose the bands of Orion?

—Job 38:31

. . . imperialism is rapidly becoming an anachronism . . .
—Pope John XXIII, *Pacem in Terris,* n. 42

When I saw the Lamb break open the sixth seal . . . the moon grew red as blood . . .

—Revelation 6:12

Why is Culture One, or institutional, Catholicism so preoccupied with the preservation and enhancement of its teaching authority? It is obviously to be expected that the leaders of a church that claims to mediate to the world the teachings of Jesus Christ, Son of God, should claim teaching authority. The magnificence and depth of its traditions, the mysteries rattling its cellar doors from within, possess, when allowed to speak for themselves, a subtle and compelling spiritual authority. If that is true, why are church leaders constantly troubled by problems in maintaining their own authority? Why is so much of their energy devoted to defending their claims to authority and exerting control over it? If what they teach is spiritually authoritative, why are they plagued with concerns about their own authority to teach it?

By being so obsessed with this issue, the official Catholic Church —the pope, the bishops, and the organization chugging like fiercely linked freight cars behind them—reveals its identification, purely as an organization, with all the other worldly structures for which authority has been the major problem of the century. The institutional church shares the blood supply of secular organizational society over against which it customarily defines itself. The church reacts in an anxious, not to say baffled, manner to an essentially structural problem. This is a signal about the worldly dynamics that energize its institutional self. But it has so draped this secular reality with supernatural gauze that it no longer easily perceives its natural character. The church, like a material building rocking along with every other building in a tremor-struck city, cannot avoid this shaking in its institutional framework. It is perfectly normal. The danger lies in misidentifying its true nature and in lacking the vision to read the experience as an authentic sign of the times. We encounter here the broken quality of a great sacrament of the eternal that has forgotten for the moment its true medium and become trapped in time. This is how, in a real sense, we now experience the mystery of the separation of heaven and earth. For this is exactly what occurs when a church, meant to be a screen through which we can glimpse the transcendent, overemphasizes its concrete institutional character.

Something has gotten under our skin during the last hundred years; the irritation has not been well diagnosed although its signs and symptoms are evident throughout society. The ages are in collision everywhere, like immense warm and cold fronts boiling up thunderstorms along the seam of their meeting. The postmodern world is bewildered about authority and confused about power. Nations that seem to have stirred from a long medieval sleep have awakened, single-eyed about power, swarming over the last decades of the century, determined to reestablish their authority. Khomeini, for example, tries to turn the clock back hundreds of years under the banners of a holy war, confounding blood-lust authoritarianism with spiritual authority. The incongruity of this leader, robed as his predecessors were centuries ago, confronting the modern world with a revivified zealot's power, provides a vivid image of time and progress turned inside out.

The same clash of ages is symbolized on the evening news as Afghanistan soldiers nestle sophisticated Stinger missile launchers against their rough-garbed shoulders to shoot down fast-streaking Russian jet bombers. How striking that the world's mightiest nations, the United States and the Soviet Union, have in the same generation been pinned down, their power leached away by primitive warriors deposited in their paths as if mystical figures in a time warp. And in the Catholic Church leaders wearing jeweled crosses, rings, and court vesture are struggling to defend a monarchical incarnation of gospel authority at the end of the century at whose beginning Europe's crowned heads fell like doomed soldiers in a Viennese operetta. The times, as far as authority is concerned, have indeed been out of joint. There has indeed been something blowing in the wind.

Perhaps the best example, for us Americans, who, since the birth of our nation in revolt against a king, have been intensely ambivalent about authority, was found in the presidency of Ronald Reagan. He was elected by a populace that, after almost fifteen years of kaleidoscopic images of burning American flags, a war lost, one president murdered, two others forced from office, and a third humiliated by Iranian hostage takers, longed for the rehabilitation of national honor and authority. But this president ended up compromising the authority that in some simplistic way he sought to restore. A man from the beginning of the century himself, Ronald Reagan crippled his own presidency and cast shadows of doubt across all governmental activities by his involvement in sending arms to Iran in exchange for hostages. He had prophesied in his inaugural that "the problem *is* government" and so indeed it turned out to be. Sixty percent of the American people concluded that, in the sad affair that shredded his own authority and depleted his effective political power, Ronald Reagan was not telling them the truth. His ironic heritage was a presidency diminished rather than enhanced in credibility.

It would be a mistake to blame everything on Ronald Reagan, for he, like many other world leaders, has lived in a historical moment that he did not understand. He has been a personification of the anomalous character of the age, an old man on the verge of a new century looking backward, trying to restore the ethos of the rugged individualism of the previous century. In a real sense, he was the old man in the moon, the moon of the nineteenth century in its last dwindling phase. Reagan was caught in something over which neither he, nor any other governmental, business, or church leader had any control. Indeed, hardly any leader, from positions as different as those of the president, the pope, and the heads of Procter & Gamble and the American Medical Association, would be inclined to accept a mythological, psychological, or spiritual explanation of their continuing problems in exercising their authority. Institutional leaders, even when they preside over structures rich in these characteristics, do not understand that their authority is intimately linked to the existence and nurturance of spiritual realities rather than to organizational reform. Institutions cannot easily heal themselves of the illnesses they inflict upon themselves; organizational solutions exacerbate spiritual woes.

What we do observe in many of these organizations is pragmatic adjustment to changed concepts of authority. Transformation, in other words, without real understanding of the core problem, and, from reviewing the literature, sometimes without any deep understanding of the solutions they have fashioned. Before we examine these reactions, let us suggest and explore the true source of much of our ongoing difficulty with traditional expressions of authority.

The Troubles of Traditional Authority

Authority has trembled violently under the impact of twentieth-century events because, like the rails miles ahead of the streamliner, it has felt the radiating energy of the onrushing twenty-first century. That is to say, earthbound authority, with all its landmarks and signposts, finds itself disoriented in the age of space that sweeps all of these away. In the universe of space into which the human future stretches beyond any imaginable measuring of it, the familiar directional orientations—up and down, out and in—no longer have any meaning. The perception of the horizon is an earthbound event; all horizons disappear in space and we are left shorn of the sweet roots that have held us to the earth, challenged to imagine what is truly present just before us, a unified and seemingly limitless universe.

God and heaven are no longer *up* there, we are no longer able to think accurately of ourselves as *down* here. If prayers do not rise as clouds of incense to a heavenbound God, then our relationship with Him, and our way of communicating with Him, must indeed be reimagined. *Any*place can be the center of the world in such a transformed environment. Indeed, *any*place is the center of our newly perceived universe. We are not, of course, yet accustomed to these notions; we do not, in a way, really know what is happening to or bothering us. It is the future that troubles us, not in the pallid terms of commercial futurists like Alvin Toffler or John Naisbitt, who speak mostly of scientific changes that have already taken place, but in the redesign of our basic spiritual geography.

This occurred once, in the fourth millennium before Christ, when men first observed the passage of stars through fixed planets and, on the basis of this, offered an imaginative construction of reality that has held us powerfully ever since. The Sumerian reading of the heavens gave birth to what Joseph Campbell describes as the "mythological field" that only now, centuries after Copernicus and Galileo challenged it scientifically, is breaking down because of our actual experience in space. The older view of earth at the center of the universe, of heaven and earth divided, was the basis for ways of looking at ourselves and of setting up what seemed to be a proper hierarchical ordering of our existence.

As Joseph Campbell observed, what seized the Mesopotamian priestly skywatchers was:

...the perception of a cosmic order, mathematically definable, with which the structure of society should be brought to accord. For it was then that the hieratically ordered city-state came into being, which stands as the source, and for millenniums stood as the model, of all higher, literate civilization whatsoever. Not economics, in other words, but celestial mathematics were what inspired the religious forms, the arts, literatures, sciences, moral and social orders, which in that period elevated mankind to the task of civilized life....Today, as we all know, such thoughts and forms are of a crumbling past and the civilizations dependent on them in disarray and dissolution . . .*

The dawning of the space age was eventide for structures that patterned themselves on the hierarchical, or pre-Copernican, model of the universe. What has been insisted upon, under different names, to support the claims of both state and church is the same, now invalid, ladderlike idea of our spiritual and material world. What in the realm of the state was termed the divine right of kings was described in the Catholic Church as a God-given hierarchical structure. This, of course, instilled great confidence in those at the highest levels of such a structure because it legitimated their claims to authority. Their authority came from *above* and so could not be challenged by persons who, by the mysterious decrees of Providence, were destined to live below.

The assuredness of ecclesiastics can be caught in the tone of the sixth canon of the Council of Trent: *If anyone says that in the Catholic Church there is not a hierarchy, instituted by divine ordination and consisting of bishops, priests, and deacons, let him be anathema.* That same certainty of status may be noted in those who defend the notion of hierarchy as an eternal truth worthy of incorporation into the creed and never, in any circumstances, to be transformed. It is still so insisted upon by many who think that, in defending that concept, they are proclaiming the nature of God's Kingdom. This hierarchical conception has been defended vigorously in recent years by Joseph

*Myths to Live By, Bantam edition, 1973, pp. 250, 251.

Cardinal Ratzinger, prefect of the Congegation of the Doctrine of the Faith, once the Holy Office. It was also reasserted by Pope John Paul II during his 1987 American visit and was obviously the concept of choice of the bureaucrats who controlled the workings of the Roman Synod of the same year.* Such a castelike structuring of the church depends on the pre-Copernican projection of a universe in which the world sits first row center, viewing a stage on which all performances of nature and history are conducted solely for its benefit.

Such an imaginative slide of reality is divided into gradations of being, descending from the highest to the lowest, from the king to the peasant, from the pope to the layperson. But this long inaccurate and unworthy idea of a divided universe did not collapse imaginatively until human astronauts probed space and were finally able to stand on the moon and allow us to look with them on television as they viewed the blue-green earth *in,* not at the center or apart from, the heavens. The unity of the universe and of human beings was reclaimed in that moment, for all divisions that depended on the separation of heaven from earth, such as body and soul, intellect and emotion, and that in the institutional church were expressed in states of life that ranged from most to least perfect, were healed for good by that perception. Buckminster Fuller's prediction that "all humanity is about to be born in an entirely new relationship to the universe" had been fulfilled.

The struggles of the current century to rework forms of relationship between the governed and the governors is a necessary side effect of our movement toward our destiny in the cosmos. For our journey into space makes us journey back into ourselves. Pope John XXIII grasped this intuitively as the pontiff who served during the momentous pioneering years of manned space exploration. He repeatedly emphasized a new sense of our human unity and, in *Pacem in Terris,* wrote presciently of the new order of human relationships that was coming into being. What he understood, at least in a general

---

*Cf. *The Tablet* of London, November 7, 1987; *National Catholic Reporter,* November 6, 1987.

way, was that this fresh start called for a new and deepened spiritual sense of ourselves.

One of the themes that Pope John XXIII is credited with introducing into the consciousness of the church was that it could no longer perceive itself as an extension of Western Europe, interpreting everything in the world according to its own experience. He stressed the sense of universality and interdependence that was necessary at a time when the world could be viewed as such from space. While other popes built on this notion, particularly in their encyclicals on labor, none of them have understood or applied this understanding to the central structure of the church as an institution. Thus, Pope John Paul II, in addressing an audience of astronomers on June 16, 1987, could, referring back to Newton's *Principia,* praise "the success of the quest for unification which is characteristic of your scientific pursuits . . . is as it were a general law of human endeavor, with a particular application also in the field of religious experience."* He could not and did not, however, discuss how this unity of human religious experience challenged the hierarchical institution of the church.

Still, this sense of our becoming what Marshall McLuhan termed a "global village" pervades the modern sense of political reality even in kingdoms as once remote, isolated, and impervious to the contemporary consciousness as the Soviet Union and the People's Republic of China. These stirring monoliths, struggling to reform their top-heavy structures of government, give clear indication of being affected by the inexorable pressures of the space age. So Mikhail Gorbachev, on the seventieth anniversary of the Russian Revolution, addressed the relationship of that revolution and today's world, saying of his new foreign policy, "This concept proceeds from the idea that for all the profound contradictions of the contemporary world, for all the radical differences among the countries that comprise it, it is inter-related, interdependent and integral."†

*The Pope Speaks, Fall, 1987, p. 302.
†New York Times, November 3, 1987, p. A13.

The essential insight, still only slowly dawning in us, disrupts old lines of authority because before we could make the journey "out there" it had to exist already inside ourselves, in the human imagination. We achieve nothing "out there" before we give birth to it within ourselves. That is why, when the astronauts were asked, on their return voyage to earth in that now almost forgotten summer of 1969, who was navigating, they could truthfully respond, "Newton." For the calculations for the journey existed in his head centuries before it was undertaken. In the same way, our great leap out into the stars leads us back inside ourselves, smashing the false idol of the human person as a clumsily divided entity in a divinely ordained caste system of being. The space age does not lead us away from ourselves but deep inside ourselves, an invitation that as individuals we have received reluctantly, for it means that we must let go of a deeply ingrained emotional orientation that we are at the center of everything. We are reluctant to explore the kingdom within us, that spiritual space that is the counterpart of the fathomless space of the universe. Institutions resist mightily because their inner structure, their organizational essence, is threatened in a universe in which hierarchical configurations no longer match or support human experience. That is, they are essentially false, in their divisions, to the deepest truths of the outer and inner universes; you cannot build those structures with that outmoded set of plans anymore.

Viewed from space, the earth's unity cannot be denied. As we move away from it, the artificial divisions, such as boundary lines and the multicolored countries of maps, fall away and we glimpse the earth as one. So, too, we not only sense the earth's unity with the universe but our own unity with each other. We are part of the astounding mystery of belonging, beneath our varied skin pigmentation and traditions, to the same family. That truth is the basis for the most fundamental religious impulse of compassion, that we share the very same longings, that we are, in the phrase of psychiatrist Harry Stack Sullivan, "much more simply human than anything else." There is something undeniably one about us that is ill-served by any and every effort to divide or estrange us. That is why hierarchies are doomed in every range of endeavor, and why new religious forms must grow organically around this seminal understanding during the coming decades.

The twentieth century has been strewn with hints and portents about massive shifts in the geological plates of history. Indeed, the scrawls on our imaginary scroll of Richter-like murmurs went out of synchronization more than a hundred years before the dawn of the twentieth century in the revolutions that shook off monarchy in France and America. Historians ascribe the development of the modern world to the Enlightenment with its symbolic enthronement of the goddess of Reason in the Cathedral of Notre Dame in Paris. The rational lining of modern times may be observed easily on the surface but the roots of that great intellectual movement are nonrational, for they can be traced to the growing failure of hierarchical institutions in both church and state to understand and husband the growth of persons in accord with their authentic experience of life. Something was experienced as out of joint at that level of reactivity —"the unwitting part" of ourselves, as Harry Stack Sullivan put it —in which moral and ethical convictions are ultimately rooted. The floodtide of scientific discovery rose on the understandings of Copernicus and Galileo, on the mathematics of space imagined in the mind of Newton. And on the burgeoning conviction in countless human breasts that the old institutions that enshrined kings and justified slavery would no longer serve. High tides, we might note, are affected, as are we, with tides of water within ourselves, by the moon.

The revolutions and struggles of the nineteenth century were a working-out of fundamental insights about a changed relationship between government and people that came to be expressed, however imperfectly, in democracy. The Catholic Church felt this pointed challenge in the tips of Garibaldi's bayonets as his troops attacked the secular power of the pope, seizing the papal states that constituted the pontiff's last claim to an earthly kingdom. This occurred, ironically enough, exactly as Vatican Council I hurried, under extraordinary pressure from Pope Pius IX, to ratify the declaration of papal infallibility.

Whatever its theological merits, the claim to infallibility had enormous political significance as it reasserted, under spiritual guise, the pope's parity with the leaders of Western Europe. It may best be understood in the long run as an instinctive defensive reaction by the pope to the deep reverberations that, on the surface, were being expressed in attacks on monarchy everywhere. The language of the definition specified, in a conscious ratification of hierarchical design, that the pope was infallible on faith and morals (over private life and public belief) when he spoke *ex cathedra* (literally, *from the throne,* as, in other words, a king invoking monarchical privilege). It may one day be argued that, in a last gasp, institutional churchmen demanded belief in a concept, rooted in a heritage of God's having the king's ear and vice versa, that was increasingly incredible.

The pope's authority was, therefore, as intertwined as the golden strands fashioned into a mace head with his position on the very top of the pyramid of hierarchical organization. This extraordinary emphasis on papal prerogatives left the role of the world's bishops considerably diminished for almost a hundred years. Vatican II is understood to have taken up the task of putting the authority of the pope and the bishops back into perspective. It did this through emphasizing a collegial interpretation of the church, that is, one that recognizes that the authority of bishops is not doled out to them by the pope but is theirs in their own right. Collegiality, reflecting the relationship of the original apostles, means that the governing of the church is not the business of an individual monarchical pope but of the pope in collegial relationship with the world's bishops.

Vatican II provided a new conceptualization of the church's authority, which, as we move into the twenty-first century, will completely supplant its badly outdated hierarchical implementation of it. At the present moment of transition tension exists, as it does in the essentially compromise documents of Vatican II, between an old idea of papal and Roman domination and a more responsible worldwide episcopate and mature national expressions of the Catholic

Church. All this, however, came not only out of rehabilitated theology but in reaction to the demise of a model of church organization that was no longer relevant or workable.

The Shifting Mythological Field

The last clustered thrones of Western Europe were overturned quickly as the new century began. It was no accident that in one of the first movies of that period the French director Georges Melies depicted a space flight in *A Trip to the Moon.* In that 1902 film, one of the first with a narrative base, the rocket landed in the puddinglike cheek of the old man who was supposed to live there. Space journeys would indeed upset our ideas of the moon and of ourselves as well. The Wright brothers, soon joined by others, initiated the age of flight not long before the *Titanic,* that grave symbol of a monarchical age, sank to the bottom of the sea, its supposed unsinkability as pierced an illusion as that of the era that was closing.

The *Titanic* has fascinated us across the rest of the century in a way that is not just explained by the sheer drama of the event. Other great ships, such as the *Lusitania* a few years later, went down in equally tragic circumstances. Why has the *Titanic* gripped our imagination so much that a widespread reaction to the French expedition to raise artifacts in the summer of 1987 was greeted with resentment and a sense that this search was sacrilegious, a violation of a vessel and a space that had become sacred to us? Indeed, the U.S. Congress began efforts to prevent further explorations by law. Why all this unless the *Titanic* has for us a special significance, still murky as the waters that swirl around it, unless, in other words, it speaks to our unconscious about meanings about ourselves and our time that we have not yet fully grasped?

We will one day better understand that the *Titanic* sank not so much in an iceberg field as in the mythological field that could no longer be navigated safely. For the *Titanic* that bore the privileged and the poor on separate levels was the last great ship of the age of the hierarchical world, and its loss was the loss of that well-ordered universe. We all traveled on that ship; we grasp that in some ill-defined manner and we want to mark the split hulk and its surrounding sands as a sacred place. We don't fully understand why on the rational level but, and this is indeed the unwitting part of it, we feel the rightness of it.

We circle solemnly above the *Titanic,* attracted and disturbed by its mystery, not as a technical problem to be solved but as a spiritual event whose meaning we cannot exhaust. We pause to mourn that moment in which all classes of passengers went down together, their distinctions dissolved in the depths, and we remember that some of each class were saved, Jonahs in a resurrection in which rank and privilege lost their meaning. This incident found its counterpoint, as we will presently see, in the explosion of the spacecraft *Challenger* almost seventy-five years later. We all rode in both vehicles, one sailing out of the past and one rising into the future, great mysteries in themselves as well as about us and our destiny.

The age of individual monarchs and their unquestioned exercise of power over millions of people was coming to a disastrous last act that, as with the *Titanic,* was marked by the slaughter of the innocent. The King of England, Germany's Kaiser, and the Tsar of all Russia, those improbable look-alike cousins, brought the era of the divine right of kings to a tragic ending. The vested lords of England, for example, saw their world of privilege washed away in the blood of their dead sons in Flanders. The preferred class went to its doom, as prophesied by the *Titanic,* in a wholesale slaughter of its first sons; the British empire slid by mid-century into nostalgic memory, its royalty presiding vestigially and powerlessly over a reordered society in a socialistic governmental experiment.

The word *Kaiser,* derived from the word *Caesar,* echoed his dominion as a conqueror. The turmoil of the long century has been in the name of working out the new relationships of people and leaders made urgent by the failure of royal hierarchical institutions to govern effectively. That a monarchical-like dictatorship came out of the Russian Revolution, and that ill-fated dictatorships arose in Germany and Italy, does not change the point of this observation. These were based on searches in the wreckage of monarchy for new and effective forms of authority. In Russia, this quest, seeking a classless society, recreated the ruthlessness of the Tsar through the reincarnation of absolute control.

Absolute control, which, like absolute obedience, is essential to authoritarian success, is also breaking down in the age of new communications, many of them a function of the new moons we have strung across the sky in satellite systems.* The age of space and the age of communication overlap each other, bonded inseparably as guarantors that the power to suppress or control information has been broken forever. News of the 1986 nuclear accident at Chernobyl could not, in the age of observing space vehicles, be contained within Russian borders. It is one of the great signals that the age of control, so essential to the preservation and reinforcement of authoritarian structures, has come to an end. The agent of all this is the future, the space age invisibly reworking our politics as well as our theology.

One of the infallible indicators of a decaying institution is its insistence on secrecy when openness would benefit it far more. The 1987 Roman Synod was controlled by a secretariat group whose members, according to the *Tablet* of London, were "fully integrated into the Curia. . . . It was the synod secretariat which insisted, and kept on insisting, on secrecy, thus negating in practice the equality and participation commended by the bishops in theory, on the basis of the joint baptism of the People of God."† The same article carries

---

*Cf. *The Media Lab: Inventing the Future at M.I.T.* by Stewart Brand, New York, Viking Press, 1987, for a popularized account of communications developments that make even these observations seem out of date. As the author said in an interview, "The important thing is that McLuhan was right. Communications media are of the essence. They're all changing now; therefore the apparatus of civilization is changing." Chicago *Tribune,* November 17, 1987, sec. 5, p. 2.

†November 7, 1987, pp. 1203, 1204.

an account of Pope John Paul's question after a luncheon at the end of the Synod, "It is a great mystery. And how do we communicate mystery?" He has the right question but his bureaucracy does not have the right answer. In this evening of the century, nothing as important as mystery can be communicated in secret. The controlling instincts of institutional bureaucrats defeat the purposes to which the institution is supposedly dedicated.

The massed signs of the disintegration of autocratic organizations is attested by dozens of unobtrusive measures. The popular British television series that ran during the decade following the landing of human beings on the moon was named *Upstairs, Downstairs* and was applauded as popular entertainment. Its title, however, reflected its dramatic presupposition of history's inevitable erasure of the hierarchically ordered society that it affectionately celebrated. Its success was due, not only to its production values, but to its speaking, even in a minor voice, to what was, in fact, occurring in the lives of all its viewers. The return to Victorian design in homes and decoration near the end of the century is another small sign of our reluctance to leave what seems the cluttered earthly comfort of that last age before human beings conquered space.

The Signs of Our Own Times

If it was the end of the age of kings, it was also the beginning of the end for the robber barons of industry, who, in fact, aped royalty in their homes, which were sometimes castles hauled stone by stone across the seas, and in their styles of living, incessantly seeking regal connections through marriages to Europe's leftover royalty. No longer would people like William H. Vanderbilt be able to say, "The public be damned!" and get away with it. Lee Iacocca is a current celebrity largely because he seems our last echo of the domineering class of entrepreneurs that seem no longer to have a place in the management of American industry. As students of corporations observe, "Many founders of modern organizations could never be hired if they suddenly reappeared. Their behavior is now inappropriate."*

The sequelae of these large-scale changes that began decades ago may be observed almost every day in one small way or another. For example, social commentators have suggested that the primary impetus for the women's movement came at the very beginning of the twentieth century, fueled by energies developed in the nineteenth to pursue successfully the vote for women. This was the first great victory for an impulse whose dynamism has continued to propel the women's movement into our own time. This movement, which has reshaped the personal and professional relationships of men and women, represents the working out of the dynamic changes that actually took place a hundred and more years ago. Various signs of this continuing transformation are everywhere in the environment. Some of these appear in new business practices, for example, aimed at recruiting and promoting more women executives, or in other experiments in modifying traditional lines of authority in factories and executive suites. Many of these efforts are instinctive reactions rather than insightful transformations and frequently represent impulses to maintain male control. Most of these moves are more superficial than profound. Still, even if not so understood, they are the outcome of large-scale changes pressing on all authority figures.

Business finds itself puzzled as it struggles, again pragmatically rather than in the pursuit of insight, to adjust to the reordering of authority that the space age forces upon it. Procter and Gamble, one of America's most successful businesses, is in the midst of changing itself in a way that unconsciously drew descriptions from the *Wall Street Journal* that fit our argument almost exactly. "Classic brand management," the account tells us, "isn't working any longer, and P&G and its competitors are scrambling to overhaul the way they develop and sell products. The result: a revolution as they alter what one consultant calls 'the most sacred of sacred cows.' " This language

*Kanter and Stein, *Life in Organizations,* New York, Basic Books, 1978, p. 8.

is unconsciously accurate in its evocation of mythological symbols, for the problem involves nothing less than tinkering with what had seemed a given in the corporation's perception and exercise of authority.

The article goes on to observe that the "comfortable world has vanished as . . . new classes of consumers . . . outnumber the thinning ranks of at-home housewives." A closer examination of P&G, the writers tell us, "illuminates the upheaval occurring in modern merchandising. . . . Consider the company's shifting organization chart. . . . Most striking, P&G's brand managers no longer operate like mini-czars but are assigned to teams with manufacturing, sales and research managers, people they once outranked." After detailing the shifts in regard to specific products, the article concludes: "Still, team spirit is proving difficult to instill at a company used to clear lines of authority. To the layers of midlevel marketing managers at P&G and its competitors, brand management 'is the Holy Grail and they're reluctant to tinker with it,' says Mr. McHenry of McKinsey & Co. (a consultant firm). Adds a P&G advertising manager: 'Sharing authority is always painful.' "*

A related story chronicled another effect of the space age registering in American business. Heralding the arrival of a "two-tier" set-up in large companies, the article's subhead proclaimed "A Requiem for Paternalism."† The account details the collapse of the American company as a total institutional environment that offered security and a way of life, ranging from health care to picnics and softball games for its employees. While economic explanations, such as increased foreign competition, are given as the reasons for these changes, it is impossible not to see that, at its core, this development reflects the broader reworking of authority that is taking place in our time. It is a wrenching and painful change because as companies surrender total control over their workers, they treat them more impersonally as well. As Eli Ginzberg, professor emeritus of eco-

---

* *Wall Street Journal,* August 11, 1987, pp. 1, 10.
†*Ibid.,* May 4, 1987, p. 1.

nomics at Columbia University, notes, the world of work "damn well is less stable. It's less stable because the world is less stable."*

What is striking, of course, is that, in addition to the mytho-poetic language about the grail the chroniclers of P&G's experiment unconsciously adopt, these tales are of inductive searches for some way to deal with an unexpectedly changed order of things. In short, these are industrial examples of everybody's problem. Perhaps P&G should have read more deeply the difficulties it experienced in recent years with its traditional corporate emblem. This display of moon and stars was thought to be a satanic symbol and caused the company such a public-relations problem that it had to be retired. Perhaps the leaders of the company would have done better to hire a mythologist rather than a management consultant to help them understand what it all really meant. What has really bedeviled them, and everyone else, is the nature of authority on the verge of the twenty-first century.

Yet another corporate effort to cope with new understandings of authority had been reported the day before in the same newspaper, in an account of a one-week seminar at General Electric's Crotonville Management Development Institute, a campus-like facility that not only develops future leaders but spreads its chairman's "vision of the company and molds a common GE culture." Simply put, it is GE's response to the problem that all great organizations are experiencing. Many other companies, including Ford, Eastman Kodak, and Prudential Life Insurance, have, we are told, "come to study the Crotonville program. One of its features is dividing managers into groups charged with solving a hypothetical yacht-disaster problem. "In each group but one, the team list (of things to do to survive) turned out to be more correct than the individual rankings. The team that didn't do as well . . . relied too much on the advice of two members who had been Eagle Scouts—and who seemed to be experts at such outdoor predicaments—instead of reaching a consensus. Besides . . . teaching consensus management, the workshop

*Ibid., p. 14.

'taught us that sometimes the expert isn't an expert . . .' " said one of the participants. Obviously General Electric, like so many corporations obsessed with finding techniques as effective as those employed by their Oriental competitors, is seeking to adjust to a world in which authority does not work the way it once did.

A Culture Two Case History: Clericalism

Clericalism provides us with a relevant example of a subculture whose molecular structure is identical with that of the massive institutional ecclesiastical culture. And just as that church culture is experiencing the same puzzlement with authority common to all large organizations, so the clergy now share with the other professions an ambivalent and uncertain grasp on authority. The shell of clericalism is badly cracked, as, indeed, are the sociological casings of medicine, law, architecture, and all other callings that lay claim to special knowledge and skill. Large numbers of professionals of middle years correctly and wearily complain that the calling in which they now find themselves, some perplexed and others embattled, is radically different from the one they chose to enter. Moonstruck, all of them.

Before examining further the modification of institutionally dependent clericalism, it is important to note that the clerical lifestyle should not be identified with ministry any more than the health-care culture should be identified totally with the art of healing. The essential defining character of each profession is distinct from the social position and esteem that it enjoys at any given time in any given country. The professions, however, have been particularly vulnerable to attack and criticism during this frenzied age of reevaluating all authority figures. Clerics are under pressure not because of a lack of faith on their part just as doctors are scrutinized not because of a lack of dedication on theirs; both groups, along with their professional colleagues, are battered by a universe undergoing a cosmic identity crisis.

The effects of this complex cosmological, mythological, and theological problem are not automatically or totally beneficial. The death of hierarchy creates a void as chilling as the one in Genesis, leveling society in some fashion, dangerously imperiling the notion of healthy authority, yielding a temporary dark night of uncertainty and confusion. The interim chaos is a Petri dish for the growth of haphazard notions, superficial philosophies, and new life for Marxist notions about "power sharing" in a harmonious classless society. In the professions, the interlude of confusion is evidenced in the attempts to reduce all professionals to the same level as those they serve, to translate their functions into economic terms, with a concomitant reduction of their social standing. Professionals in America are less tolerable as an elite than rock stars and other celebrities.

Numerous opportunistic infections may be observed as social side effects of this long moment of change. Culture One of Catholicism partially and very usefully fulfills its destiny by resisting momentous change, by using its enormous ballast to stabilize society in times of such seemingly directionless transformation. The tradition that Culture One conserves contains sound and indispensable treasures of spiritual insight that have been interred in its deepest institutional vaults. Serious analysts from Culture One do identify failed philosophical themes that echo as if freshly discovered in the superficial mottos and slogans that are symptoms of the current ongoing change. Their rattles always sound louder in suddenly empty structures.

These include, as mentioned, ideas of "empowerment" as a substitute for coming to terms with healthy authority. Hazy notions like "power sharing" imply that *no* differences exist between the learned and the unlearned, the skilled and the unskilled, and that a protoplasmic leveling of a natural (not supernatural) ordering of society is an unquestioned and unquestionable ideal. This breeds, as Allan Bloom pointed out so trenchantly in his bestseller *The Closing of The American Mind,* a universal and destructive moral relativism. The quest of the post-hierarchical society is not for primitive chaos but for something far more difficult and far less romantic, a sound and healthy embodiment of authority.

In other words, just because Culture One's complex but accidental institutional temple is crumbling, it does not mean that its essential Christian insights are no longer vital. Culture Two—this Catholicism outside the walls of the institution—grew, as we have repeatedly noted, out of the strengths of Culture One and, even as it separates itself, continues to learn from it. So, too, Culture One, shaken by the loss of its hierarchical superstructure, is forced to rediscover within itself the riches that, in its obsession with locks and keys, it has sealed away in a hiding place it no longer remembers.

The Clerical and the Medical Cultures

Perceived in one way, the clerical life has suffered what many inside Culture One of American Catholicism describe as apocalyptic calamities: the resignation of thousands of priests in the last twenty years, the decline in numbers of applicants to seminaries, the morale problems experienced by clergy, whose average age borders now on sixty. In addition, and for perhaps the first time in the memory of most Catholics of either culture, priests are no longer readily excused for their failings. Priests are not now sacred persons. Just as they may be defeated if they run for public office, so they must stand trial and endure the penalties if they are convicted of fraud, drunken driving, or child molestation. The culture no longer offers protection because it can no longer even protect itself. And Catholics of Culture Two are prepared to face the truth about their clergy without thinking that the world has come to an end. Indeed, it is important to observe that no harsh anticlerical feeling exists in the American Church: there is still a great reservoir of respect for priests, but it is far different from the uncritical acclaim that was expected of Catholics in the golden age of Culture One. Catholics have what can only be described as a Catholic attitude toward their priests— a seasoned appreciation of them as imperfect human beings.

Clericalism is to the priesthood as the gnarled shell to the meat within, the cultural sheathing rather than the essence of its theological reality. It is cracking not only from hammer blows from without but, ironically enough, because of efforts to modify its authoritarian nature from within. By instinct, institutions employ organizational notions of reform that often make things worse for themselves and the values they are meant to preserve. Institutional remedies falter because their goal is not to solve the essential problem but to preserve institutional control over the problem area. Organized medicine bears a striking resemblance to institutionalized pastoral care. They share genes that make them vulnerable to the same contemporary challenges. The American Medical Association seeks, as ecclesiastical clericalism does, to preserve the ideals of a noble calling and the sociological context in which it existed comfortably for decades. For doctors, this not only included the prestige and privilege granted to the clergy, but a vast diverse social milieu, which offered special niches and activities for doctors' wives and families.

The effort to preserve a way of life that is passing away through no fault of physicians themselves is, in the strategy and tactics of the AMA, doomed to frustration. But in order to maintain its own life and position of control in health care, the organization persists in providing *institutional* solutions that do not adequately address, or show evidence of even recognizing, the overshadowing cultural problems that render these solutions both impractical and ineffective. Ostensibly to protect its members, the AMA, in its various battles over malpractice litigation and with other health-care entities challenging its representational authority in the field, has, curiously enough, done everything but speak purely for the calling of the physician. The organization has employed classic institutional techniques, based mostly on the advice of such nonphysicians as lawyers and insurers. It has spent millions to influence legislatures and to wage public-relations battles, but, as the century wanes, doctors find their professional status increasingly assailed and their formerly unperturbed lifestyle under continuing threat.

Physicians, like priests, remain indispensable to society, and great numbers of them are respected and loved on an individual basis. Nonetheless, their general abstract positions of automatic privilege and authority in society have been notably compromised, and the once-secure cultural context of their lives is so no longer. Institutional tactics do not serve well any grand strategy to assist them. So with the clergy, many reforms quickly voted in after Vatican II were focused on issues associated with the *institutional* control of clericalism rather than the essential character of priestly ministry. These served the institution spuriously but not the individual priest. This accelerated the decline of the very cultural setting it sought to preserve.

Early ecclesiastical reform measures, for example, were aimed at correcting the abuses and distortions of authority represented by the then well-entrenched but sometimes tyrannical, seemingly irremovable pastors who ruled supreme into mummified old age. In an archdiocese such as Chicago, and in its surrounding dioceses, certain priests prized becoming a pastor as the long-awaited reward for their lives of service and sacrifice. This was the cultural expectation and was not thought remarkable in the least, for, in the popular Biblical justification, even the oxen could eat of the grain they had helped to grind.

I recall vividly a pastor from a diocese near Chicago who consulted with me during the period of turmoil that accompanied institutional reforms in the mid-sixties. A good man genuinely baffled by challenges to his authority, he described at length his average day, which, after he offered Mass, usually consisted of attending a funeral in some large parish in the Chicago area. Pastors would gather at these, lunch and visit together afterward, then make their way home by dinnertime. It was what was expected, the prerogatives of a culture that judged this to be the divine order of things, a generally harmless, mildly indulgent expression of old-fashioned clericalism. He could not imagine why his young associate complained that he was not around during the day. This particular pastor died a year or so later, a victim, I have always thought, of the way of life that collapsed on and suffocated him. His final words to me described what was happening very well. He said of his upstart curate, "And in addition to everything else, he also attacked my *monsignorate!*"

Instead of addressing deeper problems, Vatican II reformers, thinking of the church largely as a hierarchical enterprise, stressed institutional adjustments that, a generation later, have, much like the AMA solutions for doctors, contributed to, rather than relieved, the continuing problems of priests. These reformers stripped away the fragile reward system of the clerical life, limiting terms of pastoral office and doing away with the few available symbols, such as that title, *monsignor,* that could be offered as rewards for exceptional service. All this, of course, to remove the irremovable pastors, who, in themselves, were but symptoms of decay in a hierarchical system. In the long run, these bureaucratic solutions, with their efflorescence of personnel boards, provided a new and complicated set of pseudo-democratic supports for the institution that retained all effective power.

The most dedicated priests now find themselves in a clerical model that deprives them of something essential for their healthy adjustment, the freedom to live and grow in relationship to a reasonably well-grounded family of believers. Such blind "reformed" clerical rules are clearly a retouching of a Culture One notion; they place enormous pressure on the best of the nation's priests while solving a problem that no longer exists. Those who suffer most may be the possessors of Culture Two views who continue to live in Culture One. Greater love than this no man (or woman) hath.

The inexorable transforming action of the future on the church does not mean its end—the church is extraordinarily accommodating to change in the long run—and it does not mean, as previously mentioned, the complete collapse of the priesthood or of its essential sacramental ministry. Culture Two Catholics readily endorse the constantly developing forms of church ministry because they are not wedded to the preservation of institutional forms for their own sake, or to the need to control access to ministry. They do not believe that anybody needs permission to do good, and they understand atrophied clericalism as an obstacle to the implementation of the ideals of priestly service. The best evidence of their readiness for progressive change comes from an inspection of the changes that they have already accepted in the large numbers of parishes whose pastoral leadership is now in the hands of women religious and laypersons. This latter development, now recorded in official church documents —and now accepted by Culture One—illustrates how the institution itself fights reality with one hand and embraces it with the other. It is significant because it means that on the behavioral level these changes have already taken place. That suggests that they are already well advanced and cannot easily be rescinded.

The seemingly endless debates about celibacy and women priests that glow like a dim aura around clericalism will not be settled by a vote or a council; they will be resolved in a more evolutionary fashion as the weight of medieval burdens clanks to the floor like an outmoded suit of armor that has been empty for a long time. The present apparent crisis of the clergy cannot be solved through using methods that were appropriate to earlier heavily institutional periods of Catholic life. Many of the most dedicated and sincere inhabitants of the primary culture of American Catholicism are wearing themselves out trying to restore ways of life for which no restoration is possible by such means as earnest but old-fashioned vocation drives, whose meager results only discourage them further. These old institutional standbys do not match the inspiration to ministerial service that is found everywhere, male and female, and of every age group, in a de-institutionalized culture of belief.

Pathology in Professional Cultures

The documented news reports about pedophiliac priests that appeared in the mid-eighties were coupled with constant but unverified tales of extensive homosexuality within the priesthood and seminary system. In the last few years Catholics have read about their formerly idealized clergymen being arrested and going to jail for drunk driving and a variety of other problems, including child molestation. These parallel the stories of "impaired physicians" who have fallen away from their calling's ideals through drug, alcohol, and patient abuse. Lengthening shadows of demoralization fall across both professions. Similar observations can be made of many lesser professions. The newspapers are crowded with stories of lawyers, judges, accountants, bankers, and stockbrokers who have misused their positions of authority.

If we step back we can see how this is related, not to the disintegration of the ideals of the priesthood or health care, or its essential functions, but to the clerical and medical cultures themselves, the accidents of time, place, and circumstance that have nourished their substance in this country for generations. When this happens, the pathology that can be observed is probably nothing new, just the same infection that has bubbled along for years shielded by institutional walls and ways of dealing with them. When these give way, we see what has been contained if never condoned within the margins of the clerical subculture. We will never sensitively comprehend or respond to specific problems, such as that of pedophilia among priests, unless we adopt this broader perspective.

The fact that priests are no longer protected persons, excused for their misdeeds and amply rewarded for their good ones, is a sign of the restyled Catholic culture in which they function. Their vulnerability to evaluation and criticism means that they also function in the manner of other professionals. In other words, priests are now more subject to the dynamics that govern professional life in the broader American culture. As Dr. John Corbally, president of the MacArthur Foundation, observed recently, "Neither expertise nor the professions seem to be honored and our society may be drifting toward the acceptance of emotion as the primary basis for decisions." The late Mayor Richard J. Daley of Chicago once asked rhetorically, "The experts, what do they know?" These observations resonate in the clerical world as the already described search for new models of authority continues. Let us now examine how closely the complaints of priests match those of other professionals, how, indeed, professional discomfort looms as a symptom of the transition period through which we are passing.

Priests, our experts on spirituality and our sacramental mediators, live, in other words, in an age of mounting discontent among all professionals. Their complaints are remarkably similar. Many physicians, under as much stress as priests, as discussed before, find, under the pressures of malpractice litigation and the rise of entrepreneurial medicine, that they no longer derive satisfaction from what they once loved to do. Many plan early retirement, transfer to administrative or academic medicine, and discourage their children from entering the field. Despite predictions of a doctor glut, other analysts foresee a shortage in the next decade as a result of cultural developments that had not been factored into earlier projections. Physicians, perhaps not unlike priests, are scrutinized for the least possible failing or inconsistency at this time.

So, too, American architects speak with longing about the past and uncertainty about their future. *The Wall Street Journal,* for example, headlined a review of a book of interviews with leading contemporary architects with the phrase "The Thrill Is Gone," and the reviewer summed up the work as offering "a look at a profession that is, at least for the moment, without a cutting edge." A recent survey of college and university professors revealed that 40 percent of them may leave the groves of Academe within the next five years. Twenty-five percent are considering entering another line of work, not surprising when 40 percent explain that they are less enthusiastic about their careers now than when they began. Close to 30 percent said they felt "trapped" in their jobs, leading the Carnegie Foundation to judge the profession to be "deeply troubled."

A December 3, 1985, article in the *New York Times* asked, "Is the science of chemistry fading away?" and quotes John Maddox, editor of *Nature:* "Chemists have done wonders in losing their identity in the rest of science." Changes in the scientific culture, in other words, have transformed this profession, leading the *Times* to conclude, "Truly, the science of chemistry seems to have lost its identity." A few weeks later, in a feature story in the same newspaper entitled "Why Today's Orchestras Are Adrift," conductor Leonard Slatkin, observer of changes in the classical-music culture, concludes, "In a sense we no longer know whether we're doing it right . . . we can't go on this way." The article notes that musicians are "very concerned. They are aware of the question of keeping their souls intact amid all the expansion of activity and income."

Even recipients of prestigious Fulbright scholarships, through which they become experts on other countries, complain, according to the *Chronicle of Higher Education,* that they "are ignored when they come back to the United States." Nurses, according to the Chicago *Tribune,* still "get no respect." The same complaints about professional identity and gratification rise from accountants, lawyers, high school coaches, and law-enforcement officials. Even a prosperous California farmer recently announced that he was giving it up with the complaint, "It's just no fun anymore." Early in 1987, the *New York Times* ran a feature on the collapse of the town-meeting tradition in New England.

But enough. It is clear that many of the problems of the Catholic priesthood are identical with those of other moonstruck callings. Whatever specific difficulties they may have as individuals, they will necessarily be subjected to increased stress because of this reality. Whether we are reworking our professions for good or for ill is not certain. It is evident, however, that all those who profess to know more than others in our culture, all those claiming to be of a special class, are being roughly challenged to reestablish their right to cultural recognition.

The trembling on the surface of American life is evidence of the significant changes at a deep level that are occasioned by the break in our geographical and spiritual sense of continuity by our leap into space. We have, uncomfortably but without awareness, been trying to live on that desert margin caused by the separation of heaven and earth. In rediscovering the unity of the universe we rediscover that of our own persons as well; we have the chance to see into ourselves and into the spiritual depths of the world of appearances. But this enormous expedition into the kingdom that is within us is not easily mounted or undertaken; we would be surprised if we did not experience these current dislocations in our sense of time and space. The problems of the clerical subculture, as those of medicine, are only small aspects of this broader and inescapable change. Viewed in this richer context of understanding, we can avoid panic, the use of outmoded institutional solutions, and indulgence in depressing prophecies about the end of the world. The true end of the world occurs when we comprehend the extraordinary unity of heaven and earth.

The Catholic Church, with its incredible institutional inertia, withstood the impulse to abandon authoritarian structures longer than most entities. Vatican II, an event in a historical process rather than in itself a cause of anything, marked that moment in which the church, searching out an older tradition, rejected authoritarian structures and replaced them with collegial processes. This change, so absorbing and energizing for the first Catholic culture, actually means the end of much that is familiar and endearing in that revered culture. We are witnessing the disintegration of cultural forms that were dependent on the integrity of the authoritarian structures inherited from another age.

The most striking public symbolization of this change took place in the very heart of the regal ceremony once known as the papal coronation. Pope John Paul I rejected the tiara, the triple crown, in favor of a stole of pastoral service; his successor, John Paul II, did the same, signifying a sea change in papal self-understanding. That Pope John Paul II kisses the ground of the lands he visits is a further, somewhat more subtle if slightly histrionic, gesture that he arrives not as a royal personage but as a pilgrim. Both symbols are still overpowered by the abundant surround of ceremony, but they remain germinating slowly within the royal panoply, and will gradually purge it of its presently overpowering authoritarian character. Most of the world's bishops would not be against this. It is also true that most do not now realize that they wear medieval court dress, which represents the very authoritarianism that the papal stole of service eclipses as a symbol of their authority.

We are, then, moonstruck and the cloud of seeds blowing steadily off the top of the next century has already taken root almost everywhere we look. The church, unlike most other great institutions, had a rich tradition of collegiality, into which, with fine theological justification, it is gradually reinvesting its authority. But even the church is not undergoing this without the pain and struggle that attend every birth. The period of transition, during which we have clearly sensed the tension in every human institution, has been marked by trial-and-error adjustment, by experimentation, and by pragmatic rather than enlightened acceptance of new lines of authority. The church has not listened to or trusted its own poetic depths during this time. It might have recognized its own wisdom, a wisdom, we might add, beyond the control of administrators, that lives its own mysterious life within the church.

For example, the church might have appreciated that in the mid-century definition of the dogma of the Assumption of the Blessed Virgin, that is, that the Mother of Jesus was assumed bodily into heaven, it was speaking mystically about the age that the world was entering. We will allude later to the way metaphors, essential to the language of true religion, are destroyed when they are treated as concrete historical realities. It is enough here to recall again psychiatrist C. G. Jung's observation that the definition of the Assumption was the most important religious event of the period because it symbolized the return of Mother Earth to the heavens. In other words, while on the level of Culture One the church was putting its official stamp of authority on the dogma of the Assumption, the mystical church, that of Culture Two, was prophesying the reestablishment of the unity of earth and heaven, the beginning of a new age and a new sense of ourselves.

The official church might also have paid more attention to its own rich symbolism, not the least feature of which is the moon. The moon, liturgically, religiously, and mythologically, is the timeless symbol, as it sheds its own shadow to emerge as new again, of life shaking free of death, of eternal life. The moon in its fullness after the Spring Equinox marks the celebration of Easter, the return of light with the illuminating sun and the illuminated moon in the sky. The moon, in the church's own usage, represents life conquering death, the old waning and the new waxing, the very central mystery of death and resurrection that, as an institution, it experiences and resists, blind in its organizational eye to what its mystical eye sees clearly.

9

A Case of Mistaken Identity

Authoritarianism Against Authority

You have heard it said . . . But I say to you . . .
                                                    Jesus in the gospels

O, what authority and show of truth
Can cunning sin cover itself withal.
                        Shakespeare, *Much Ado About Nothing,* IV, i, 36–37

An X-ray of the twentieth century reveals a shadowy growth running from the top to the bottom of its lighted frame. The invading illness splays into finely infiltrating threads at one point and bulges like a fist at another as it closes its sinuous, choking embrace on the healthy organism. Thus pathological authoritarianism has entwined itself with healthy authority in a prolonged struggle that has spread tension across the century. As in any sickness, the balance between these forces shifts constantly, and we may view clearly the contesting elements found in all stressful human experience, the *pathos,* or suffering, and the *ponos,* or struggle for health. These abiding features may be discerned throughout the decades of pain that have been marked by massive efforts to forge new relationships between people and their leaders as well as with each other.

Culture One of Catholicism, along with every other community in transition, is gripped and obsessed by its need to preserve its authoritarian, controlling reflexes. Culture Two Catholics, on the other hand, are disengaging from the battle itself, leaving the illness behind, like persons who realize that it is healthy to move out of the moldering old castle into the fresh air and sunshine. Culture Two is shifting its center of gravity into the broad open fields of the future, while Culture One's strivings mire it more deeply in the past.

The long struggle of these hundred years has involved authority's search for expression in a world that has left its kings behind, many of them murdered, all of them dethroned, their faded glory a bittersweet memory at best. This zigzag, violent, disordering pursuit has been filled with false starts, huge disappointments, and enormous confusion and anguish. People have overthrown tyrants at one moment only to long for their return in the next. More than once the liberator has transformed himself into the dictator. It has not been unusual for men and women to seize freedom only to find, as Camus once observed, that it "is a long distance race . . . quite solitary and always exhausting," and that the responsibilities of autonomy are "too heavy to bear." In this present twilight of the hierarchical domination of human existence, Americans feel uncertain and ambivalent, sensing that they know better what they don't want from authority than what they do.

Damaging healthy authority in order to overcome authoritarianism, like the dust-filled razing of a patriotic statue in the town square, is hardly a constructive outcome for any institutional entity, including the Catholic Church. The long revolt against authoritarianism has, however, often harmed healthy authority. The restless century has not been in love with anybody's being in charge anywhere for any length of time. The undiscriminating virus has infected authority, competence, and most instrumentations of order and restraint, threatening in its yeasty explosion of cells to obliterate all signs of health. The indices of most social-science research volumes, such as *Psychological Abstracts,* list dozens of investigations of the evils of authoritarianism but hardly any on the nature and function of healthy authority. We enjoy diagnosing the illness we feel deep in our bones but we act at times like patients who prefer being sick because we are afraid of the responsibility of becoming well. There are, as with sickness, secondary gains to an ongoing battle with authority, gratifications of primitive, anarchic impulses that we do not wish to surrender.

Culture Two Catholics, like all Americans, chafe under authoritarian structures. They do not identify blind obedience, the response not only demanded but considered holy by autocratic ecclesiastical leaders, as intrinsically sacred. Their reason for rejecting such a compliant and unquestioning reaction arises not from some impacted contrariness against all authority but from their intuitive good sense, from the best part of themselves, the healthy instincts whose authority Thomas Aquinas urged human beings to trust. These Catholics shrink back from pathological demands on their personalities in the same way that healthy people are repelled by unhealthy efforts to seduce them into an opinion or behavior that goes against the grain of their basic soundness. Healthy persons feel what philosophers term the "out of jointness" of propositions that, howsoever nobly rationalized, make them objects of another's needs. That reaction against manipulation is a sign of health, a signal given by the personality that is a reliable guide to moral judgment and action. This reluctance to hand themselves over without question to the control of others is, therefore, not obstinate truculence but operational good sense. The authority within Culture Two Catholics is, in such cases, healthier and stronger than authoritarian persuasions from without.

Many Catholics in Culture One also refuse to obey the contaminated authority of the still heavily bureaucratized sections of that culture. They must, however, make some kind of adjustment to these death-throe reactions of the monarchical institution in which many of them serve as priests and religious. They look away from or do not invest in authoritarian efforts to control them or the Catholic people in general. The pastoral mode allows them to temper old-fashioned totalitarian religious strictures so that they do not become impossible burdens or, for that matter, sharply contested issues among the ordinary people to whom they minister. Even First

Culture bishops, intensely and unquestionably loyal to the institutional church, preserve what they can of their authority by not spending it on hard-edged efforts to extract blind obedience from their people on issues over which genuine differences of opinion exist. They approach the church's teaching on birth regulation, for example, as pastors rather than as authoritarian leaders, responding with a sacramental-like sense of their flock's need for understanding rather than condemnation on such difficult matters of conscience.

Such convictions and reactions do not flow from the refusal of such Catholics to accept the idea of authority but from a guileless search for an authority that is credible to them. This does not signify a flabby, protoplasmic authority but one whose expectations are rooted in and matched by genuine understanding of their life experience. The decision by many Catholics to form their own consciences on such issues as birth regulation is not, as some institutionally based critics claim, a hedonistic option but rather their knowing assumption of a serious moral obligation. That Catholics decide for themselves on serious moral matters is evidence that they understand the most traditional and authoritative Catholic teaching about the ultimate criterion of individual conscience. Forming their consciences after examining church teaching and tradition and inspecting the concrete reality of their own experience is not a simple or effortless task. Through such a reflective approach these persons give evidence that they take their obligations seriously. They do not, however, take seriously institutional churchmen who deride or fail to value their assumption of moral responsibility for their own decisions.

Mature believers in both cultures of Catholicism recognize the sensible place of healthy authority in any well-ordered or productive human life. Culture Two Catholics do not believe, as some anarchists do, that life can be improvised in a spontaneous and impulsive fashion. That is blind obedience to an inner tyrant. An authoritative life, one that commands our attention, flows from the person's disciplined and consistent effort to listen to the feelings that are shaped by and resonate to the deepest and most finely wrought moral convictions. Impulsive actions, exemplified by acting out on the basis of rage or lust, corrode the soul, ultimately destroying the individuals and their relationships, rendering them barren. Mature lives, in which authority is a well-integrated concept, are generative, enlarging individuals and enriching all their relationships.

Although we can readily describe and list the attributes of authoritarianism, it is far more difficult to do the same for authority. Healthy authority, as with health in any of its manifestations, pulsates with mystery, with that never measurable and ever elusive quality that inheres in every fully alive person or fully lived moment. You cannot close your hand on it or trap it. A close parallel exists with physical health, which always cloaks itself in mystery, a step ahead even of physicians.

Handbooks are crammed with diagnostic categories for every sickness. Thus classified, individuals are no longer defined in terms of their own personalities but according to the syndrome they inhabit with others. A measure of their individual wonder and mystery is thereby subtracted. Persons diagnosed as having AIDS may quickly find their individual personalities, their once-in-history lives, submerged in the dread of shapeless illness; they are stricken in more ways than one, for they are quickly perceived as "cases" more than as themselves. On the other hand, we have only the term itself to describe health. The reason, of course, is that health is manifested only in individuals. To understand it, one must look at and listen to its possessors, each of whom reveals health in a distinctive and non-duplicable manner. Such singular vitality is powerful and finds no adequate synonym in such a term as "wellness," as pale an image of the real thing as "togetherness" is of genuinely loving family life.

Human beings are as thoroughly spiritual as they are totally and indivisibly human and physical; these elements cannot easily be pried apart even for purposes of analysis, or one creates, as institutionalized religion and materialistic science often have, a deformed creature unworthy of the name human and hardly recognizable as such. Unfortunately, the model of the person still embraced by many Culture One church administrators is that entity divided hierarchically into good and bad parts (*partes honestae et inhonestae* as old moral-theology manuals termed them), in which the soul strives to escape the sinuous, entrapping strands of the body. This unhealthy model of human personality, however, is the mirror of the church as a many-tiered presence and, for many institutional churchmen convinced of its eternal reality, rationalizes their confident authoritarianism. This unhealthy model of the person also justifies unhealthy strategies of control and manipulation.

What if we followed ordinary good people as trustworthy guides to what is humanly and, therefore, religiously healthy? We would find revealed the world of sensible and morally good judgment. Ordinary good people are practical moralists. They possess common sense, that is, that "sense of the community," the *sensus fidelium,* that even the official church has always acknowledged as a reliable moral guide. This sense of the faithful has been identified in theologian Patrick Granfield's research as one of the traditional balances to the excessive use of papal authority in the church.* Granfield argues that "because the faith lives in the faithful, their reception of papal teaching is significant, and the possibility on non-reception and dissent comes into being."† The sentiment of believers, then, is a vital indicator of the soundness of even a pope's pronouncements.

A related axiom, buried in the archives of the institutional church and largely forgotten by bureaucrats, is also a healthy and valid guide to moral judgment. It suggests that, if we are in doubt, we may follow what the *sanior et major pars fidelium,* the larger and healthier majority of believers, does in a certain situation. Sensible decisions flower out of sensible lives. So, in turning toward healthy people for guidance, we encounter a commonplace mystery and follow Christian instincts so deep that their expression has been consistently honored, even in the most thickly bureaucratized eras of church history. Culture One, whether its leaders remember it or not, has always respected the instincts of healthy persons, conferring on them operational authority in the realm of personal morality.

*The Limits of the Papacy, New York, Crossroad, 1987.
†Peter Chirico's summary in Commonweal, November 6, 1987, p. 634.

One cannot, as we will presently find with Catholic novelists and their work, ask healthy people to explain their health to us. Self-consciousness in the pursuit of either physical or spiritual health leads to similar results: single-minded, asocial, hollow-cheeked runners and saints with goals and lifestyles very different from those of ordinary persons. Genuinely healthy people are not much concerned about the achievement of appearances; freedom from such anxiety is an aspect of their healthiness.

Indeed, a lack of self-consciousness about their own goodness seems to be a consistent characteristic of healthy people. In no passage of the gospel is this clearer than in the story of the last judgment, which has so frequently been distorted into a terrifying tale of God's shaming vengeance on sinners. The real point of the story is not that persons' sins will be revealed but that their goodness will be recognized. Strikingly, those invited into the kingdom "prepared from all eternity" cannot recall the events for which they are being given spiritual credit. When, they ask, did we see you naked and clothe you, or hungry and feed you, or discover you in jail and visit you? They cannot remember for a very simple reason: they were not thinking of themselves or of the impression they would make when they gave of their time and energy to other persons. They saved themselves in those moments in which their concern about themselves was minimal. That is the way holy, healthy people are.

Love is not blind; indeed, it is attracted to these homely indications about the richness and diversity of the beloved. As in all the myths, it is where we stumble and fall that we discover the gold. And, as the pastoral church well knows, healthy people are also sinners; we could never otherwise appreciate their goodness. Nothing is more deeply anchored in the Catholic tradition than a feeling for human beings *in via,* on pilgrimage, moving forward, getting up after falling down, their health made clear only because of the fall, after which they rise and move forward again. Health and holiness belong to such seekers of the grail; the meaning resides, of course, in the seeking more than the finding. Absolute perfection is a false god, the father of idolaters. What is healthy is grander, simpler, and, of course, more mysterious and more congenial to human beings. It is observable every day in ordinary people, not in their cholesterol counts or blood-pressure readings, but in their natural, unstrained way of being human with each other.

Healthy authority is, therefore, manifested not in efficiency of control but in the enlarged, unaffected lives it helps to build, *in,* as St. Paul wrote, *caritate non ficta,* love that is without pretense. Authority comes from the Latin word *augere,* which means to increase. This is the taproot of *author,* the sturdy source of nourishment for its essentially generative and creative nature. Those in authority, such as loving parents, make it possible for their children to grow. The concept is almost a polar opposite to the unhealthy authoritarian urge to control and supervise strictly, and thereby to diminish the lives of others. Healthy authority obviously understands the need for correction, discipline, and sensible order. Its feeling for these, however, is integrated with a fine and balanced sense of what contributes to the human good of the other, to what, in other words, builds the true character of the child, student, or believer. Those who employ authoritarianism, however, are not interested in the good of others as much as the gratification they derive from imposing their will on them.

Healthy authority is not a construction based on some detailed master plan. It is implemented in one everyday moment after another in a fresh, spontaneous manner; that is health's only design. Its hallmark is love, affection if you will, rather than intimidating fear. Healthy authority reveals itself in a genuine appreciation of human personality, in wonder and reverence for the mystery of existence, in respect for individuality, and in a personal readiness to make sacrifices for the good of the other. Even this process is not without risk, but, in general, wholesome authority humanizes persons, enhancing them spiritually, opening them to the world and its wonder, and to the intrinsically religious nature of existence.

Culture Two Catholics—those who see their faith as a way of life rather than an exacting organizational membership, believing that the institution exists for them and not the other way around—understand that belief and religious practice can be tested in a simple and infallible way. Faith and its implementation are structurally unhealthy if they employ unhealthy means or lead to unhealthy outcomes; they are pseudo-religious at best and cannot be Christian in any sense. The old adage *corruptio optimi pessima*—the worst comes from the corruption of the best—is fully applicable to such distortions of religion.

Any spiritual plan that divides the human person, igniting conflicts between body and soul or intellect and emotions, is, has been, and always will be unhealthy. That misconception and consequent maltreatment of human personality are passing away along with the institutional religious concepts of a graded spiritual life that went with them. Culture Two Catholics simply turn away from authority that perceives them as divided persons; there is nothing in that view to attract or maintain their attention. Religious leaders whose teachings on sexuality, for example, remain based on this riven model of personality thereby lessen their credibility and, therefore, their teaching authority. This latter claim to authority is not diminished by rebelliousness on the part of second culture believers but by the deep structural faults in its imagery of human experience.

Before examining some recent cases that illustrate the healthy reactions of Culture Two Catholics to unhealthy Culture One authoritarianism, let us review these contrasting notions. Genuine, or healthy, authority is rooted in love, while authoritarianism bases itself in fear. Perfect love, Jesus reminded his followers, casts out fear. Authoritarianism is not interested in surrendering control while authority does so as subjects in relationship to it acquire self-control independent of any outer vectors of reward or punishment. Authoritarianism leaves no room for trust, that margin of freedom in which others are left on their own. Authority knows that, even placing everything thereby at risk, it must trust in order to be trustworthy.

Faith, the scriptures proclaim, "comes through hearing." The word obedience comes from the Latin *ob audire,* which means *to listen to.* Listening is the natural response not to an abstract command but to the substance of a personal message. Such attention strongly implies human presence and exchange, and, therefore, a reciprocal relationship whose attractiveness and effectiveness derive from its own organic qualities. Human beings turn spontaneously, even in casual conversation, toward others who seem to understand or make sense of their experience for them. Men and women do not give this profound natural response, however, to those who speak in clichés that betray a lack of comprehension of their experience. They may put up with such persons but they cannot be compelled to *listen to* those, especially the immature or insensitive preachers who insist that they do so. Watch good people during boring sermons and you will discover the large repertoire of responses they use, such as cleaning out their purses or reading the Sunday bulletin, as they wait out the preacher.

Blind obedience is an interesting concept that reveals the internal weakness of authoritarianism. By its nature it bids human beings to close off their senses. Perhaps that is necessary in the rigors of war or under the pressures of disasters, but it fails completely as an expression of spiritual values and realities. The principle of contradiction is involved in expecting people to be both human and blindly obedient. Persons cannot shut off their senses and remain humanly and spiritually alive. Faith does come through hearing but only if there is something worth listening to. Persons who hear someone make sense out of their lives and experience freely give their attention, stamping as valid the authority of the speaker.

Authoritarianism depends on depriving its subjects of their senses, in refusing to let them see, hear, or inspect the trustworthy internal soundings healthy people regularly experience as assessments of the believability of others. Indeed, authoritarian church leaders have systematically insisted that persons should disregard their personal reactions, override them, treat them as idle and misleading flappings of the psyche that would only lead them to grief. When human beings could still be made to feel guilty for a sin no greater than being human, this violation of personal integrity in the name of religion was commonplace and served institutional ends very well, at a high cost to individuals. Most so-called spiritual tracts on obedience emphasized what subjects would get out of twisting themselves out of shape to accept and carry out even the most irrational directives. Never mentioned was what authoritarians got out of giving such orders and watching people follow them. Authoritarianism is essentially ordered to the preservation and expansion of hierarchical power, while authority primarily pursues the integrity and growth of persons as members of the human community.

Many ecclesiastical administrators have confused the teaching authority, or the church's *magisterium* (a word, interestingly enough, derived from one that means *he who is greater*), with their outmoded hierarchical construction of both the universe and the church. They now defend that concept, thinking that they are protecting healthy authority, which, in fact, they are thereby damaging severely. Culture Two Catholics do not obey—they literally do not *listen to*—authority when it speaks in this ancient, defensive, and unpersuasive language. This is a healthy reaction, not arising from perversity, wantonness, or rebelliousness. This judgment is the acid test, the sound reaction of the *sanior et major pars fidelium,* the wholesome appraisal by believers of those who claim authority over them. If authority, like faith, is also tested through hearing, the fact that ordinary good people no longer listen to authoritarian pronouncements is a profound and telling revelation of the latter's hollow character and outmoded style.

Genuine authority promotes spiritual insight and enhancement, always bringing more of other people into being, leaving realistic room and freedom for the organic growth of their true personalities. Of such is the everyday setting for religious mystery, that transcendent quality that suffuses the simple but heightened moments of life. Mystery is not meant to be confounding but enlarging, not a blinding flash but the gentle, steady light by which men and women can see more deeply into themselves. Mystery inheres, for example, in lovers' first recognition of each other, in their being faithful to each other, in their facing and sharing the truth not as a weapon of confrontation but as an opening to a cleaner, uncompromised, and intensified relationship with each other. There is more of people in existence after such experiences than there was before.

Mystery lifts off every human transaction in which people give something out of love, even if it is only a small consideration, a wise understanding, or a generous forgiveness. Sometimes it is something as simple as not saying something when words of any kind would only make the situation less bearable. Such familiar, even homely, incidents carry unmistakable authority; they arrest our attention, stir our imaginations, move and transform us in a positive way. Religious bureaucrats are not meant, through insisting on their authority, to manage these simple moments of transcendence but to recognize and support them, thereby helping people to grasp their sacramental significance.

Ordinary people do not find their basic religious experiences inside churches but in the course of their daily lives. They go to church to be reminded of the spiritual meaning of what they experience outside of it all week long. Genuine church authority, therefore, is essentially sacramental rather than controlling or supervisory in nature and function. Popes and bishops imbued with a sacramental sense of the world never insist on or argue their claims to authority. When they manifest a feeling for the religious character of human experience, believers readily vest them with authority. Such figures fulfill the calling of good shepherds; they know their flocks, and their flocks know them. Authoritarianism, on the other hand, closes people off from themselves and each other, rejecting sacramentality or marking it down, overemphasizing an external, highly controlled kingdom rather than the spiritual kingdom within persons.

Authoritarianism mocks genuine authority, especially in its willingness to use power against vulnerable persons. Seeking conformity rather than free commitment, it lacks any capacity for self-observation as it employs low-level techniques to repress and control its subjects. Authoritarians in the church employ the psychological equivalent of the devices of the Inquisition in attempts to compel or monitor religious belief or behavior. Defenders of so-called "orthodoxy" have, throughout history, been single-eyed in inflicting salvation on people by force.

True authority is intrinsically sexual in nature. It is ordered to the enhancement of human relationships between flesh-and-blood persons; it is, therefore, thoroughly generative. Authoritarianism remains static and barren. Authority awakens, speaks to, and respects sexuality in persons, calling forth what is authentically masculine and feminine without false uneasiness or excessive self-justification. It is comfortable with human persons, integrating them with, rather than alienating them from, their sexuality. Authority's metaphor is healthy sexual union while that of self-absorbed authoritarianism is masturbation fed by sado-masochistic fantasies. Authoritarianism is the whitened sepulchre filled with dead men's bones spoken of by Jesus. Jesus's chief targets were corrupted religious leaders who perpetuated their minute control of people's behavior through managing a hypocritical religion of obsessive external regulation. Authoritarianism always settles for making something look good; it thrives on stylized and superficial imagery, that is the manipulation of the appearances of life. It is terrified of the unmistakable authority of things as they are.

Authoritarianism, especially as used by certain Culture One administrators, is, as we will explore in the next section, asexual in its motivation, emotionalization, and manipulation of people. Without allowing itself to observe or ponder the implications of its actual goals, such authoritarianism frequently employs techniques of ridicule and shaming, playing on the sexuality of persons in a denigrating manner, in order to bring and keep them under its control. Authoritarianism thus debases and diminishes others in order to gratify the pathological needs of those who exercise it. These latter wielders of power substitute this manipulation of people for the healthy sexual expression that they fear and avoid.

10

Sickness Against Health

The Asexual Core
of Institutional Authoritarianism

Try hard to make yourself worthy of God's approval, a work-man who has no cause to be ashamed, following a straight path in preaching the truth.

—II Timothy 2:15

He was not born to shame. Upon his brow shame is asham'd to sit.

—Shakespeare, *Romeo and Juliet*, III, ii, 91

David Tracy's observation that "the only people who are not afraid of the Catholic Church are Catholics" marvelously captures the affectionate family spirit that, perhaps uniquely, still characterizes their Church. Culture Two Catholics feel that they, rather than an institution silhouetted against a blood-red medieval sunset, constitute the church as the movement and the way of life founded by Jesus. Many Vatican disciplinary initiatives during the eighties, however, caused profound distress for those who understand the church this way. This included bishops, priests, and religious men and women whose lives are lived in Culture One although their hearts are in Culture Two. The most notable were the removal of Father Charles Curran from his position as a Catholic theologian at the Catholic University of America, and the disciplining of Archbishop Raymond Hunthausen of Seattle, whose authority was awkwardly dismantled in an action that lasted more than a year. It is *how* these incidents occurred that unsettled good Catholics, who felt that people simply weren't treated that way in a family, that some sacred territory of the spirit had been violated by an approach whose true nature, like that of a cattle brand, could be read in its smoking signature on flesh. In short, many healthy American Catholics were convinced by these and other incidents that gave evidence of similar motivation and intent that something basically unhealthy had happened to them. And they were right.

No matter how these interventions in the American Church were intended, they were experienced as classical asexual assaults meant to shame and humiliate good people. Catholics could smell the burning lime in the wind, and they pulled back in shock as it splattered on them while being heaped on others. What had been done in the name of authority and unity had actually brought a curious division; what was supposed to be medicinal, as Culture One church administrators call their punishments, did not heal but violated the spirit.

These cases provide excellent examples of those trustworthy reactions of Catholics (the *sanior et major pars fidelium,* the healthier majority of believers) to which we have already referred. This healthy majority may have been the original definition of that second culture of Catholicism, which includes, along with great numbers of laypeople, many bishops, priests, and religious who remain inside the first culture. Not extremists, they constitute the great moderate center of the American Catholic Church; they keep the world and the church going. Their feelings are not only reliable guides to moral judgment and belief but they are also filled with information about events that rouse them. Here we encounter the *sensus fidelium,* the sense of believers, not as an abstraction but as the reliable, living responses that arise from the everyday common sense of the Catholic community. The widespread anguish of millions of Catholics suggested that they perceived quite accurately the unhealthy objectives as well as the level of gratification associated with such Vatican administrative procedures. Culture Two's healthy intuition was that pathology had clearly invaded the institutional aspects of Culture One and that, because of its nature, it was both easy to recognize and to distinguish from the Spirit's gentle breath in the People of God.

If we examine our own experience we can identify moments in which we have failed and been justly corrected by parents, teachers, or pastors. The ones we remember, those elders we recall as truly helpful in our development, always tempered their correction with understanding. They made us feel that although we might have fallen short of our true possibilities they loved us anyway, and that we were still valued in their eyes. We can also recall people who, in the name of helping us, humiliated and embarrassed us instead. We know that their own inner needs, rationalized on the surface, were being gratified, that we were being used, abused actually, for their self-centered purposes. The latter, however, could not admit what they clearly communicated: their need to dominate, to "put us in our place," and to "keep the upper hand." In short, a game of domination.

Similarly, we appreciate a person's attempts, with honor and integrity, to uncover a difficult truth with us. The process, even if we attempt it by ourselves, may be hard but it is essentially ennobling, a measurable triumph of life over death. We also understand clearly when another person, in the name of revealing truth, is really manipulating us, using us slyly, visiting us with a small death, diminishing our life instead of enlarging it.

If we trace the origins of the pain these sensible Culture Two Catholics experienced as a result of institutional discipline, we find that it arose not as the price of uncovering hard truths but as the corrupted result of being spiritually debased. The underlying institutional dynamic, recognized or not, was indeed that of asexual assault, marked by strategies of degradation, on good people. It was intrinsically asexual because of its failure to be generative and because its term was not enlarged human relationship as much as the exercise of self-referent and self-gratifying power. Asexuality is so named because it characterizes those who rationalize, often theologically, abusive activities that are a substitute for adult sexual relationships of which they are incapable. Such asexuality does not seek communion; it is blind to family values, to the building up of the young that is the hallmark of a sound community; it is phosphorescent, as explosive and self-consuming as a match head, and its blind nature is fulfilled in its burning.

We feel it whenever a self-satisfied authority figure condescends to us, whenever, for example, a bland churchman betrays an estrangement from healthy sexuality by confidently but awkwardly making harsh or ill-timed judgments about this sensitive subject in the lives of others. Classical church careerists seem hypnotized by some erotic blaze, see only by its light, and make a ruin of their authority by struggling endlessly to control others through tactics that gratify but also reveal their hunger for domination. Perhaps this Richelieu Syndrome develops in any organization that becomes so absorbed with institutional purposes that the enhancement and preservation of its power begins slowly to seem the same thing as its service to others. Any hierarchical structure that is endowed with great power over human beings—and that includes governments, schools, and businesses as well as churches—has the potential for mistaking the saving of its structure for the saving of others.

Even as spectators at the Curran, Hunthausen, and related incidents, many good Catholics who deeply love the Church felt that they had been unpleasantly manipulated out of some dark but powerful institutional urges to maintain control and to keep up the appearances of propriety and righteousness at the same time. To such sensitive believers in the late eighties, the Kingdom of God seemed to suffer manipulation and the manipulators were bearing it away.

There were repeated episodes in which corrupt dynamics manifested themselves unmistakably. Several took place within one calendar year. A young girl was humiliated publicly by a church official who would not allow her to be confirmed because her mother worked in a birth-control clinic. Another young girl was similarly shamed and expelled from grammar school because she had participated, according to her mother's sentiments, in a pro-choice march. A Jesuit priest who had discovered in a survey of the American bishops that a substantial minority held liberal views about celibacy and married and women priests was ordered to destroy the results or to resign from his order, as he subsequently did; another priest who had written a book about ministering to divorced Catholics was forced to leave his diocese; superiors of religious orders were urged to crack down on opinions expressed by their members; nuns who had . signed a pro-choice letter that had appeared in a national newspaper two years previously were tracked down systematically, some found serving the poor in Appalachia, another on the missions in South America, and were told that they had to recant or face further disciplinary actions; a 1986 Vatican document on the pastoral care of homosexuals belied its title by its harsh and unforgiving tone; throughout the country, at the urging of Roman authorities, groups of homosexuals were forbidden to attend special Masses in Catholic churches; certain archbishops forbade ex-priests who had not been officially laicized from receiving the sacraments at the hands of understanding pastors.

Each of these incidents caused good people to wince because, intended or not, each was perceived as an excessive and self-righteous use of power against highly vulnerable targets. These actions did not clear the air but left it tingling with the acrid smell of shame. Healthy people instinctively stepped back; there was something wrong, and it was not with them.

Added to these multiplied examples was the long interrogation of Father Charles Curran about his carefully modulated writings on birth control, divorce, and homosexuality. Perhaps, as many observers noted, Vatican discussions with Father Curran were careful and mannered and, yes, perhaps if we had known everything that went on behind the scenes we would have judged this matter more generously. But the Catholic community's perception was that Father Curran had been made an object lesson because of pastoral theological opinions that were hardly revolutionary or unique, that a signal had been given, and that, stripped of his credentials to teach Catholic theology, Father Curran had been cast into a shadowed exile.

But does the gentle, pastoral Father Curran really seem like a threat to the people of God, does his willingness to listen as patiently as the Curé of Ars to the confessed struggles of the divorced, homosexuals, and those in conflict over birth control make him a dangerous example for priests and bishops? How many people, including true sources of public scandal, such as corrupt businessmen, government officials, and outright criminals, has the official church treated with such absolute certainty of their wrongdoing? Why, if over seven hundred theologian colleagues supported him, was Father Curran disciplined? The main charge seemed to be that he dissented from what the Roman teaching authority (here read *authoritarianism*) was willing to allow on subjects related to sexuality.

The Curran affair, however, did not stir the central ranks of the Catholic community as deeply as the earlier announcement that Archbishop Raymond Hunthausen of Seattle had been relieved of his authority in five areas that had been taken over by a newly appointed auxiliary bishop, Donald Wuerl. Once again, insiders reported that there was more to the story than we knew, and, at one point in its tortured course, Archbishop Pio Laghi, the Vatican nuncio, revealed his own chronology of the investigation of charges of pastoral and administrative neglect brought against Hunthausen.

Made public, they seemed neither like mortal sins nor the wildly disobedient actions of a bishop challenging church authority in any way as flagrant as those of the French Archbishop Marcel LeFebvre. The latter had called Paul VI a heretic and rejected Vatican II's decrees on religious liberty and ecumenism. He had set up his own wing of Catholicism, ordained his own priests, and threatened to ordain bishops, had been suspended by Pope Paul VI in 1976, but was dealt with subsequently in a very delicate manner by church officials, apparently to avoid the very kind of embarrassment they were willing to heap on Hunthausen. This truly disobedient prelate was treated as if he were a prophet of some absolute Catholicism of which most Catholics were not worthy. In short, the manipulators were manipulated in 1987 by a pious master of the art, LeFebvre himself, who was able to maintain ready access to the Vatican and personally worked out terms of reconciliation that he would later cast aside, without any apparent disciplinary actions against him.

Vatican expert Desmond O'Grady described Lefebvre's actions as "blackmail," and suggested that, in granting him "generous" terms for reconciliation that might allow him to retain his outlaw seminary and occupy a "personal prelature (a diocese without frontiers)" the Vatican "may be seen as being afraid of having any enemies on the Right. Cardinal Ratzinger . . . could be seen as accepting Lefebvre's viewpoint rather than Lefebvre that of the Vatican."* Lefebvre's remarkable success in manipulating Vatican officials who have dealt with Curran and Hunthausen as if intoxicated with self-righteousness may be a function of his understanding the true foundational dynamics of Culture One. The disenchanting lesson may be that Lefebvre speaks the bureaucrats' language fluently; he knows their hearts, their asexual vulnerability. He knows, in other words, how to work his will on them, humiliating the humiliators, an expert at emasculation, wearing a red mantle.

Curiously, Hunthausen, whose full powers were restored in May 1987, remained loyal and responsive to the Holy See throughout his period of censure, ever the attractive and guileless human being, who was constitutionally incapable of being other than straightforward and nonmanipulative. When examined, his offenses seemed to be the pastoral judgments of a large-hearted Christian. Indeed, they reminded one of the quotation from Péguy of which Pope John XXIII was fond: God does not ask much from men, only the heart.

Fair-minded people could not discount the unsettling impact of the chronology of events supplied by Archbishop Laghi because its spirit and tone were unmistakable and were picked up by outsiders who were not looking for them. Joseph Berger of the *New York Times* noted that the document "was studded with references that

Our Sunday Visitor, October 25, 1987, p. 21.

could embarrass the archbishop [Hunthausen]." And Bruce Bu-
ursma in the Chicago *Tribune* observed that "The Vatican's version
of the story depicts Archbishop Hunthausen as a truculent and du-
plicitous bumbler." What came across unambiguously to two non-
Catholic religious journalists was the effort, however unconscious,
to lessen esteem for Hunthausen, to triumph by demeaning him.

Archbishop Hunthausen had always impressed the Catholic community, even though some of its members disagreed with him on
certain issues, as a true pastor and a real man. Those who knew him
identified these qualities as genuinely, unself-consciously his. That a
good man, on the basis of accusations whose makers had been guar-
anteed confidentiality, was perceived as emasculated and left to founder publicly struck a deep and discordant note in the soul of the
larger and healthier portion of the Catholic community. That the
same extreme right-wing letter writers who took credit for bringing
about the Hunthausen investigation by their complaints to Rome
publicly exulted in his humiliation revealed clearly the low-level
satisfactions they had sought and achieved for themselves.

The Hunthausen case came to symbolize, as Archbishop Francis
Hurley of Anchorage, Alaska, noted, the "state of the Church." It
displayed prominently the institutional game plan of asexual debase-
ment so at odds with the authentic church's sacramental sympathy
for and embrace of sinners and stumblers. It was not just Culture
Two laypeople who reacted with discomfort to such tactics. Thousands of healthy priests and religious as well as the majority of
American bishops felt great sorrow in their hearts because the perverse nature of these interventions violated their own pastoral instincts and practices. Such people strive to use their own sexual
celibacy constructively in authentic generative services to the community. They felt severe pressure as a result of Rome's actions
toward Hunthausen because they were themselves humiliated by
them.

The American bishops were caught in an uncomfortable bind, for
they would have been judged somehow disloyal unless, in effect,
they implemented directives, the tenor if not the intent of which was

pathological. American Catholics, as loyal to the Pope as any other of the world's people, or more loyal, experienced the Hunthausen disciplining as a hot iron in their own souls that further estranged them from administrative officials, who seemed insensitive to the techniques they employed, as they always claimed, "for the good of the Church." This made the eventual collegial resolution of this case the most urgent pastoral mission of the American bishops in the winter and spring of 1987.

A great many American Catholics were repelled by these efforts to achieve ecclesiastical control through variations on the themes of shaming and humiliation. As the November 1986 meeting of America's bishops approached, such Catholics were on the verge of concluding that the institutional church had somehow put the salvation of itself ahead of that of its members. Many also felt that if U.S. church leaders failed to stand up and stand by their brother, a good man who, whatever his faults, was transparently a conscientious Christian, the bishops themselves would become additional victims of the institution's capacity for intimidation and control.

The first casualties in the Hunthausen case were, cruelly enough, the men who had earnestly tried to serve the institutional church's purposes. The Apostolic pro-nuncio, Archbishop Pio Laghi, was hardly unaffected by the complications of the very situation that he sought to mediate. Bishop Donald Wuerl had accepted a difficult assignment only to find himself whipsawed by events that were beyond his control. Everybody later agreed that it had been a monumental blunder to give him the assignment in the first place. Against the background of the sordid affair these well-intentioned men stood out like figures in a Le Carré novel, victims of the dark side of the institution to which they had given their lives, sacrificial offerings to the demands of blind loyalty to the "company" purposes.

The 1986 Vatican document on the pastoral care of homosexuals proved to be a classic example of the excessive use of shaming and humiliation in dealing with human beings. Many people criticized Pope Paul VI as a Hamlet of indecisiveness in his reflections on the church and the world. But many longed for his anguished tone, so tempered by an appreciation of the ambiguity that inheres in everything human, as a redeeming contrast to the enormous self-confidence, if not arrogance, that marked this set of guidelines. How scalding they were to men and women who, along with many heterosexuals, struggle every day to understand and come to terms with their sexuality.

It would be difficult to imagine a series of statements more destructive to the already imperiled self-esteem of homosexuals than the ones in the official paper from the Congregation of the Doctrine of the Faith. Not only were homosexual-rights groups not to meet or to conduct worship services on church property, but individual homosexuals were reminded of the "evil" of their actions, and, in the most condescending and degrading of all assertions, were told that "the particular inclination of the homosexual person . . . is a more or less strong tendency toward an intrinsic moral evil; and thus the inclination itself must be seen as an objective disorder." Vatican officials did not seem to understand that almost all human beings experience homosexual impulses at one time or another in their lives. Only those who are excessively sure of their own moral purity seem able to cast first stones without caring where they land or whom they hurt.

This was obviously embarrassing to the strongly pastoral American bishops, at whom, according to some interpreters at the time, these guidelines had been specifically directed because of the understanding positions they had supported or tolerated in dealing with homosexuals. It placed pastors and teachers in a difficult if not impossible position, as indeed it did anyone with a feeling for human frailty. This was, therefore, the complete instrument of humiliation because it not only shamed homosexuals but placed those who ministered to and attempted to understand them in a shadowed and suspect position as well. How gratifying it was for those whose pleasure came, whether they recognized or admitted it, from dominating and defeating others in the name of defending virtue. This asexual emotionalization, intertwined with the self-satisfaction some right-wing extremists felt at the moral plight of homosexuals, was easy to identify in their hostile, sarcastic, and self-righteous tones. Such newspapers as the St. Paul–based *Wanderer,* which has consistently supported any and every effort to debase those it has opposed over the years, including many leading bishops, revealed the biting harshness of spirit that certain Culture One Catholics mistake for devotion to orthodoxy.

Healthy people understood that this set of instructions, and its delighted supporters, "protested too much," that its assertions and its judgmental style were out of proportion to the problem that it was supposed to address pastorally. Why, good people wondered, were Vatican officials so upset about homosexuals? These guardians of orthodoxy did not seem nearly as morally outraged about terrorists, drug smugglers, or munitions dealers as they were about these men and women who, it must be remembered, were trying to preserve, not break, their relationship with their church. One need not endorse homosexual practices in order to deal with homosexuals in a manner that acknowledges and supports their basic human worth. And what is a church as a home called to offer its children if not a welcome in time of pain and distress? A home, Robert Frost once wrote, is "the place where, when you have to go there, they have to take you in." The Vatican document seemed to regard homosexuals as outcasts so basically flawed that they had to be expelled from the community. Was there a place, Culture Two Catholics wondered, for any of us who so clearly bear the marks of original sin?

The lack of grace with which some Vatican officials deal with issues connected with human sexuality has led to a perverse seamless garment that is a true cloak of shame. Would it not be better, Culture Two Catholics asked, to strive to reach out in relationship to another person, as many homosexuals genuinely do, than to remain forever asexually isolated from friendship and love, as many of their harshest ecclesiastical critics seemed to be? Church officials might well ponder this question, for a position that systematically rejects any effort to love on the part of a certain class of persons renders itself literally incredible and destroys the authority of those who support it. It is intrinsically unbelievable; it commands no obedience, alien as it is to genuine human experience, and, therefore, falls on deaf ears. In debasing others, such bureaucrats debase themselves. To remain locked inside the self is not an acceptable moral alternative for any Christian. To imply that homosexuals harbor some inner stain of character that makes them unfit for even chaste relationships of friendship is a misreading of psychology and common sense and a serious distortion of the basic command of Christianity. Smug asexuality that perceives itself above all human intimacy, cannot be the ideal of any living faith.

Hard-core Culture One Vatican administrators should seriously examine the exaggerated zeal of their crusade against homosexuals, exploring the implications of the frequently reported clinical findings of experts that many church personnel lack a clear idea of their own sexual orientation. Such persons report that they are either undeveloped emotionally or that the controls of church structures have so impinged on their lives that they have not achieved any real sense of their own masculinity or femininity. They have cruelly been made eunuchs for the institutional kingdom. Absolute control, which is clearly the issue in these incidents, exacts a high, demeaning, and ultimately dehumanizing price from those forced to submit to it. Culture Two Catholics, free of the demand of bureaucrats to accept their rationalizations of unhealthy authority, pull farther away from the structures which, filled with such pathological dry rot, seem poor housing for them as a People of God.

Culture Two Catholics love the church and the pope. They are not out to overthrow either, but they will not put up with the institution's small side, with its diminished sense of values and its clerical preoccupations. It was of Culture Two that Avery Dulles wrote a decade ago, "Many Catholics have lost all interest in official ecclesiastical statements and do not expect any light from the magisterium on their real problems."

What was ultimately remarkable about these many corrosive incidents was the healthy reactions to which they gave rise. These did not come from some highly organized campaign. A tide of feeling rose swiftly in the second culture when the efforts to shame and permanently humiliate Archbishop Hunthausen seemed near success. The healthy response to this unhealthy use of authority was found in the sadness that permeated the American Catholic community, sadness that was appropriate to the occasion, sadness that prompted an assessment of the losses that could be sustained without incurable alienation setting in. To its great credit, the National Conference of Catholic Bishops followed its soundest instincts in an orderly and pastoral request to reexamine the Hunthausen situation. This healthy reaction led, through the efforts of a committee of bishops, to a successful mediation of the affair and to a restoration of Hunthausen's faculties as a bishop and his dignity as a person. This was not achieved through rebellion but through collegial cooperation and with a purpose not to shame or defeat any of the involved parties, including its Roman institutional sources. Health, in the long run, triumphed in a manner that enhanced the authority of America's bishops and strengthened the faith of its people. It reinforced the self-confidence of Culture Two Catholics as well. It was a major and decisive example of the effectiveness of the kind of authority that is intrinsic to healthy religion. The peaceful and constructive resolution of the Hunthausen affair also made it clear that Culture Two Catholics are defined better as a family of peacemakers than as a commune of revolutionaries or selective believers.

And what did the institutional churchmen learn? Their greatest tragedy would be to misinterpret reactions to the Curran, Hunthausen, and other incidents as challenges to their divine-right authority. Something very different actually occurred. Culture Two Catholics can still love Culture One's officials even as they condemn the evils of officialdom. The latter do not yet seem to appreciate that in their attempt to restore a kind of last-century authority they compromised the possibility of their having any real authority in the next century.

11

Strangers in a Strange Land

Authority and Human Experience

*Then I saw new heavens and a new earth. The former heavens
and the first earth had passed away. . .*
—Revelation 21:1

Theory is all gray, and the golden tree of life is green.
—Goethe, *Faust*, Part One

Science has been depicted for more than a century as St. George,
slayer of the dragon of religion. In the popular mind and, indeed,
among more sophisticated people and scientific entertainers such as
Carl Sagan, science has plumbed the void and found it a desert
without God's footprints, a drear emptiness through which superior
beings hurl signals at us as the gods once did thunderbolts. It is as
if scientists have been enjoying revenge for the church's pyrrhic
victories over such ancestral colleagues as Copernicus and Galileo,
overturning the tables of the dogmatists and driving them out as
righteously as Jesus did the moneychangers from the temple. Religion, its quaint stories of creation exploded by geological calculations about the age of the universe, was no longer seen as a vital
influence except, perhaps, among eccentric fundamentalists, who
spiritedly defended the historical accuracy of the Bible against what
were termed the assaults of "godless scientists."

But what kind of religion crumbles under the pounding of the scientific battering ram? And in what battle are fundamentalists joined as they summon up literal interpretations of the end of the world in purifying fire? This continuing skirmish, which now identifies "secular humanism" as a co-conspirator against religion, is reflected in incidents concerning the use or banning of textbooks, the teaching of creationism as well as evolution, and in intra-sect battles over the interpretation of the Bible. Meanwhile personalities like Sagan have become confidently dogmatic purveyors of a new orthodoxy that continues to regard religion as outmoded. But are we talking about either religion or science as they really are?

A closer look reveals the falseness of this apparent Armageddon, in which the God-fearing peer through the barbed wire at the legions of the godless. The encounter resembles a re-creation of a Civil War battle, a reproduction that gratifies its present secure participants, bolsters their spirits with the fantasy of a fight that is endless and harmless. The actors are getting something out of it even if the pageant does not reflect true history. So, too, with science's claims to have superseded faith. Science did not destroy faith but it did inter the long-dead trappings that had been proposed by institutional religion as the authentic embodiments of belief. On the other hand, what fundamentalists have attacked is not true science but science as a swaggering caricature of inquiring and sensitive human intelligence. The combatants do not see each other clearly but they love the noise and smell of battle; nor does either grasp, as they raise their swords for another weekend charge, their own nature very well.

Science did not in any way challenge or subvert the authority of the churches. It did tear away the no-longer-supportable staging that had obscured the true nature of religious belief. More than that, science, far from explaining everything to itself and by itself, has actually reopened the formerly clogged pores of mystery, discovering the tentativeness of its own measurements, observing the universe as more complex than it had imagined and more mysterious than it could imagine. In other words, through its advances, science, like some great archeologist of the soul, has freed the essentially spiritual human personality from the bindings by which the institutional church had muffled and controlled it. Science has, in fact, entered the universe and found it profoundly mysterious.

Those institutional religious leaders wed to literalist understandings of the scriptures perceived science as endangering the concrete hierarchical construction of the universe upon which their authority rested. They sensed that, should scientists discover its pervasive and inescapable ambiguity, their world would slip out of their control. Science was branded as inimical to faith when it was actually the enemy of authoritarian superstition disguised as faith. Science, burdened at times with its own social framework, was not the enemy of but the vehicle for the questing human spirit. The religion overturned was that of insistent and unyielding literalism, whose Bible the declining William Jennings Bryan defended at the Scopes trial in 1925, the nonambivalent scrolls clamped firmly in the teeth of fundamentalists. That religion makes no room for mystery; lacking mystery it is no religion at all.

Those scientists who scoffed at faith had an exaggerated sense of their own capacities as well as an undeveloped appreciation of the abiding spiritual dimension of human beings. Scientists often did not understand religion or theology any more than theologians understood them. They therefore found it easy to knock down the straw men they propped into place for target practice. Science is a way of knowing the universe whose authority depends on a correspondence between the maps it sketches and the subjective human knowledge of the same physical and psychological territory. Religion's authority is built on a similar base. If the models it proposes about our moral and spiritual experiences do not match them, its authority collapses. This is the result not of attack from without as much as from weakness within. So, too, art seeks to hold up symbolic renderings of our experience in order to further our understanding of it. The tension between certain literal forms of organized religion and genuine science and between those forms of organized religion and genuine art (which may be described as unorganized religion) are identical in nature. Authentic religion, on the other hand, is perfectly comfortable with both true science and genuine art.

Indeed, false religion, fake science, and spurious art share the same defective genetic makeup. The real transformation of this last century has distinguished these latter ghostly imitations from their genuine counterparts. Confusion results when pseudo-religion is pitted against real science. But ordinary persons can tell the difference by comparing the model of human experience inadequate religion offers with their own personal knowledge of it. Simply put, when the preacher, of whatever denomination, offers good people an explanation of their experience that does not make sense to them, they lose faith in him, in what he says, and in the institution he represents. They also gain confidence in their own judgments about their lives and decisions. A quack scientist compromises his own authority in exactly the same way, by offering a supposedly scientific explanation, such as a model of a flat earth, that is contradicted by the experience of his listeners. Neither can the artist who offers a false picture of human nature make a valid claim to authority.

What do we mean when we speak of this "human experience" against which ordinary persons ultimately measure the interpretations other people give them of their lives? We speak, for example, of experience as a teacher, suggesting that it is classroom, campus, and tutor rolled into one. Experience, we are also told, is what we lack when we are young, and what we have had too much of when we are old. Experience is firsthand knowledge; it refers to that which we undergo or suffer; it is all of these, but what is it? In one way, experience is that field of reality on which we discover and etch the truth about ourselves. In certain systems of personality theory, experience is that of which we can become aware, or, in the labored language of psychology, that which we can symbolize in our consciousness. In other words, experience is everything which we can, like Adam viewing the animals, name rightly for ourselves.

Experience comes from the Latin *experiri; experiment* and *expert* arise from the same root. It means *to try out,* or *to test.* The expert, of course, is the person who has tried something out thoroughly. One of the suggested antonyms for the noun is *theory,* and for the verb, *to miss.* The Indo-European root of *experience* is related to a large family of words suggestive of journeys and passages, efforts and risk. The most relevant root is that which means *to try,* or to *learn by trying.* The same root anchors *periculum* to its meaning of *danger,* and appears itself in *peril;* these tell us the natural condition of trying anything out. *Experience* is a mysterious word, for its inner dynamism propels it just beyond our easy reach, allowing it to float there as something we understand but cannot fully explain.

The moon is made of green cheese, someone tells us, but our experience on journeying there tells us something else. The earth is below, the heaven above, we are told, and yet when we experience them from a perch on the moon we find that this is not so either. Experience is what we know through our own senses, that to which we are eyewitnesses. St. John appealed to it; he had woven his gospel of what he had "seen and heard." So, too, St. Paul spoke almost passionately of only wanting to tell his readers "what we have seen and heard." Jesus offers experiential proof of his teachings—the deaf hear, the blind see, the poor have the good news preached to them. Go and look, he says, try it out. Through our experience we are bound to what is real and undeniable about ourselves and our world. Experience is the irrefutable source, for the reasonably healthy, on which we stake our claim to authority about our own existence. By reference to what we have seen and heard we can compare and thereby test explanations of our lives given to us by others. Because of my immersion in my experience, I can judge whether these explanations match it or not. If they do, they are persuasive; they possess authority.

Growth in religious faith, or, for that matter, in life in general, demands that we pass through a succession of crises. We constantly surrender the simple explanations that serve our innocence but retard our maturity. If we do this successfully, we preserve the essence of some construct such as Santa Claus while surrendering him as a historical figure. We ultimately give up a child's version of God and come to examine carefully, as we shall shortly see, the faith that we inherited from our parents. An increment of psychological stress accompanies each of these steps; absorbing and integrating the religious concepts that reflect accurately our experience is not easy. But the very nature of growth demands that we stretch ourselves, that we find new interpretations that do fit the growing subtlety and variety of our experience. Wise parents, teachers, and other guides, along with the storehouses of our cultural tradition, enable us to make purchase of our expanding experience—to deal with love, cruelty, rejection, disappointment, and death in ways that match the profundity of these common events. We name them, refining the philosophical or religious explanations that best interpret them for us. All along the way we breathe the familiar atmosphere of experience—trial, risk, and danger.

Religion is the deepest source of explanation about our human experience. It is a resource richer than we know, a river whose water runs deep but rises, flowing over our existence, cleansing the doors of our perception so that we can grasp ever more clearly the meaning of our lives. That is what religion does when it washes freely over us, when we can, as did the cripples in the Bible, let it purify us as we stand unself-consciously in its flood. But, as with real rivers, dams may be erected, the force may be restrained or diverted, the torrent's nature tamed by its controllers. So it has been with religion subjected to excessive institutional management. When that happens, it loses something of its wonder, becomes sluggish and polluted, corrupted by its masters so that it becomes an agent of corruption itself. Religion is then a ghost of itself, bereft of its sacramental vitality as it is shriveled into a deadened and deadening literalism that can be readily monitored and supervised by institutional guardians. That kind of religion loses its power to explain our experience; it loses its authority at the same time.

That is how the Christian way of life, the good news, by nature spiritual, sacramental, symbolic, and mythological, has been hammered into the intellectual propositions and formulas of organized religion. This represents a translation of poetry into brutal prose, enlarging the distance between experience and its mirroring in faith, and finally lessening the authority of those who claim the divine right to carry out these operations. Culture Two Catholicism has developed because of the gulf that has grown so wide between the controlled institutional version of faith and its members' genuine experience in everyday life. Scientists have not challenged and destroyed such dogmatic authority; it has made itself incredible because its models of life fail the test of a fair comparison with life itself.

At a fork very like that in Robert Frost's poem, ordinary people went one way and institutional churchmen went the other. And that indeed "has made all the difference." In this century that separation has been most notable over issues connected with human intimacy, with the experience of love and sexuality. Dozens of surveys have revealed that most (read here, Culture Two) American Catholics do not accept the official church's teaching on birth regulation and, indeed, form their own consciences on a range of significant associated issues. Some observers, as noted, interpret this as an example of "cafeteria" Catholicism, in which people pick and choose what they like from the array of teachings before them. That, however, is the view of the cafeteria manager, a classic organizational assessment that blames others for the difficulties it generates itself. If the food doesn't sell, blame the customers. Even in cafeterias, ordinary people often demonstrate better instincts than the dietitian about what is good for them.

The overused and inappropriate cafeteria analogy implies that Catholics must accept everything the institution presents or else fail in their faith. That makes institutional authority the sole test of religious fidelity. But the expressions of institutional authority must themselves be tested, as we have noted, before they can be blindly accepted as authentic interpretations of the most important human experiences. And it is precisely here that many organizational interpretations of life—of sexuality in marriage, of the nature of the relationship between the sexes, of the nature of reciprocal marital responsibilities—travel on that divergent byway that leads ever farther away from the path of the true experience of men and women.

Authority that does not stay close to what actually transpires within and between people in ordinary existence soon loses credibility. Such pseudo-authority does not become incredible because of a fault in the character of believers. Failing to correspond to genuine experience, it manifests its own intrinsic unbelievability. The threat of punishment cannot stir up guilt in good people who have learned to trust their own reactions more than other people's faulty translations of them. This is the crucial testing ground for Culture One's authority. When, for example, officials argue, against the opinions of almost all theologians, that women must be barred from the priesthood because they cannot "image" the male Christ, the argument is essentially unconvincing because it does not address the crucial test of our experience, in which women seem richly gifted for priestly tasks. It imposes a theory (the antonym of experience) that is tortured and at variance with what we know firsthand. Those who offer it thereby compromise their own authority. Such a flimsy rationalization of what a male-dominated institution wants to do, knowingly or not, to preserve its own power hints at the ancient widening faults that run deep and jagged in its structure.

When ordinary people describe those authorities in whom they have confidence, they describe them more often as understanding than as commanding. We spontaneously recall those who have led us to greater growth as possessors of this quality of grasping and expressing our experience without embarrassing us. Experience, as we observed earlier, is defined by some personality theorists as constituted by those aspects of ourselves and our behavior of which we can become aware. What, in other words, we can symbolize in our consciousness so that we can recognize and possess it as part of our personal identity. This is particularly important to all of us in the areas of life about which we can be shamed or ridiculed, those tender, ambivalent, easily crushed dimensions of personality that, despite all our wisdom and research, nobody fully understands.

Our human identity is, for example, linked sensitively to and reflected in our sexual feelings and reactions. We are far more assisted by—and are thus far more inclined to listen to and to trust

—those who seem to understand our struggles from the inside rather than by those who sit in judgment on us, in the devil's various superficial guises, which range from the ecclesiastical inquisitor to the *Playboy* adviser, telling us how we should feel and be instead of respecting how we do feel and are as flawed, growing persons. That is why, in fact, ordinary people listen more to Ann Landers, who claims no authority beyond human understanding, than to some experts who display elaborate credentials but display little of her commonsense comprehension of experience.

Understanding resembles a spiritual anointing, for it strengthens us to meet the challenges of growth. It truly confirms us. Authority, as we have observed, means *to make able to grow,* and so it is essentially a function of understanding rather than of controlling or manipulating. It is clear that the sacraments are meant, at least in part, to be instruments of human understanding. They reflect and respond to the key points of human growth and change, reflecting life's ever-dangerous possibilities, to which they speak symbolically and mysteriously; in short, humanly and profoundly touching the spiritual core of the experience of becoming adult, marrying, sinning, or facing and bearing illness. That is the kind of authority that the sacramental Catholic Church does, in fact, possess. Often, however, its administrators fail to communicate any sacramental awareness of the human condition, thus obscuring the true nature of the church of which they are but stewards. Indeed, they seem more concerned with the discipline of the sacraments than with their purpose. Recall, for example, the prolonged debates among the American bishops in the early seventies about the acceptability of receiving communion in the hand. It remains a sore point among certain extreme right-wing Catholics, who are clearly obsessed with control over the accidentals of the sacraments rather than with their powerful function in responding spiritually to the needs of men and women.

These same Culture One controllers are also the masters of shaming and ridiculing, the techniques of manipulating others for rationalized theological ends that actually gratify their own stunted and distorted sexual appetites. Authority has been put at risk in Catholicism by many of the very officials who claim to be defending it. There is no mistaking their real intentions when they seek the unconscious erotic rewards of domination over other persons as a substitute for healthy heterosexual relationships in their own lives. Despite their denials, indeed, their rage at being so accused, they communicate their real inner authoritarian desires in what are, in truth, sacrilegious forays into the most intimate and sensitive facets of individual lives. This leaves an enormous spiritual chasm between such Culture One institutionalists and the Culture Two People of God. This radical separation in their respective understandings and approaches to ordinary life explains how authority collapses when it drifts so far away from a feeling for human experience.

The rediscovery of the experiential path of religious truth has been described by countless men and women throughout history. It is a mistake to think that it is the easy way out of burdensome obligations. The easy way is always to take somebody else's hand, to accept his or her pace, itinerary, and goal without ever asking a serious question about it. The easy way is extraordinarily painful for persons who have felt, for example, the manipulation of their own sexuality by institutionally minded provocateurs of shame and undeserved guilt. Catholics, such as those of Culture Two, who choose to examine authoritarian religious claims to see if they match the deepest layers of their experience subject their true moral fiber and their own spiritual character to the most exhausting of tests. That is the road of experience.

Culture Two Catholics have found their way to the true mythic path on which they recognize their own experience in that of all true lovers, that is, they understand that they are undergoing for themselves what every person has had to suffer in the name of genuine love. They respond to Tristan and Isolde freeing each other by the power of their love. They feel inside themselves the pain and sacrifice that, instead of easy pleasure, have always been the hallmark of the loves strong enough to challenge death and to move humankind. The story of Heloise and Abelard catches well the conflict between experience and authority. It was, according to the late Joseph Campbell, perhaps the world's greatest scholar of mythology, one of the epic signs of a world in transformation. Of that time, he writes:

> Love was in the air in that century of the troubadours, shaping lives no less than tales; but the lives, specifically and only, of those of noble heart, whose courage in their knowledge of love announced the great theme that was in time to become the characteristic signal of our culture: the courage, namely, to affirm against tradition whatever knowledge stands confirmed in one's own controlled experience. For the first of such creative knowledges in the destiny of the West was of the majesty of love, against the supernatural utilitarianism of the sacramental system of the Church. And the second was of reason. So it can be truly said that the first published manifesto of this new age of the world, the age of the self-reliant individual, appeared at the first dawn of the most creative century of the Gothic Middle Ages, in the love and the noble love letters of the lady Heloise to Abelard.*

That love parallels the experience of love that illuminates the lives of men and women today, the same experience from which institutional Culture One churchmen remain fatally estranged. Administrative ecclesiastics thought, of course, that they had effectively destroyed the love of Heloise for Abelard through the use of their immensely powerful and controlling machinery. The maimed philosopher was reclaimed by the institutional church; for him, salvation depended on his return to the safety of the supervised ranks of the clergy. The experience of the human love of the man and woman was thought sacrilegious in itself; its power was misunderstood and underestimated then, and the power of such love continues to be misunderstood now. That is why it is treated as nothing but dangerous sexual pyrotechnics that must be extinguished at all costs.

*The Masks of God: Creative Mythology, Vol. IV, New York: Viking Press, 1968, pp. 54–55.

The question that bursts still out of genuine human experience is: what does it mean for man and woman to fall in love? What happens to the woman who gives her heart to a man who can always rehabilitate himself by rejoining the clerical ranks even in the shame of sackcloth and ashes? We witness here the awesome estrangement from a central and perhaps essential human experience, falling in love. The rejection of this possibility fits the pre-Copernican construction of the universe, in which Grace floated like a precious sanctified layer far above the plain of ordinary earthly life. The rapid decline of the pre-Copernican model makes it possible for persons to see and feel the unity of their experience once more. We can, in fact, feel the tension of our present experience in the last letter of Heloise to Abelard, ten years after he had rejoined the clergy and she, for his sake, had entered a convent.

> Tell me one thing, why, after our conversion, commanded by thyself, did I drop into oblivion, to be no more refreshed by speech of thine or letter? Tell me, I say, if you can, or I will say what I feel and what everyone suspects: desire rather than friendship drew you to me, lust rather than love. So when desire ceased, whatever you were manifesting for its sake likewise vanished. This, beloved, is not so much my opinion as the opinion of all. Would it were only mine and that thy love might find defenders to argue away my pain. Would that I could invent some reason to excuse you and also to cover my cheapness. Listen, I beg, to what I ask, and it will seem small and very easy to you. Since I am cheated of your presence, at least put vows in words, of which you have a store, and so keep before me the sweetness of thine image. . . . When little more than a girl I took the hard vows of a nun, not from piety but at your command. If I merit nothing from thee, how vain I deem my labor! I can expect no reward from God, as I have done nothing from love of Him. . . . God knows, at your command I would have followed or preceded you to fiery places. For my heart is not with me, but with thee.

As Campbell remarks,

> In her own words—and they may yet be crowned in Heaven
> as the noblest signature of her century—not the natural, animal
> urgencies of lust, not the supernatural, angelic desire to glow
> forever in the beatific vision, but the womanly, purely human
> experience of love for a specific living being, and the courage
> to burn for that love were to be the kingdom and glory of a
> properly human life.*

In Abelard we discover the man overwhelmed by and transformed
into the mouthpiece of the institution that had successfully reclaimed
him. Now safely distanced from the woman he had misused, he can
defend himself, and increase her shame, through an overintellectual-
ized response. He composed a prayer of abstract pieties, in which he
asked God to pardon their crimes and to cover their faults with
mercy. It is the quintessential institutional response to human experience that is too intense and vivid, far too great a challenge for it to
be dealt with directly. Abelard bade Heloise farewell, having ignored the urgency and depth of her love, misusing her yet again
without any understanding of it, setting the stage for centuries in
which Heloise would always be sent away, in which it would always
be easier for the institution to reject than to deal with the implications of the most moving of human experiences.

Was it not echoed, I thought, in the gruff, dismissive statement of
an American archbishop when he was asked in the early seventies
about the rule of celibacy? He said, "Priests merely want to exchange their power over the body of Christ for power over the body
of a woman." No comment I have ever heard better captures the
ignorance and devaluation of human experience that has eaten away
at ecclesiastical authority's claims to our attention on any matters
concerned with love, friendship, or sexuality. Culture Two Catholics
will not and do not accept this abysmal failure to recognize and

*Ibid., 59.

understand the simple and essential elements of a healthy life. Many of those who dwell in Culture One recognize and try, especially through pastoral interventions, to make up in concrete situations for what the official church still treats shamefully in the abstract. The recovery of church authority by Culture One depends not on Culture Two's blind obedience but on its own stepping back into the waters of human experience, there to be cleansed and healed, its senses restored so that it can see and touch the real world again.

12

Thomas Merton
Died for Our Sins

Authority and Art

I am the way, the truth, and the life . . .

John 14:6

*Artistic growth is, more than it is anything else, a refining of
the sense of truthfulness. The stupid believe that to be truthful
is easy; only the artist, the great artist, knows how difficult it is.*

Willa Cather, *The Song of the Lark*

As previously noted, the two cultures of American Catholicism may
be distinguished in terms of the voices to which they listen. There
is presently considerable overlap in this regard, another function of
Catholic education's reclamation of the humanistic tradition of
which the church was once the unexcelled champion. The American
Catholic as philistine, the self-assured censor and skeptical derider
of all that was new, is not now an appropriate stereotype. If Culture
One no longer excludes any but the most pietistic of artists, Culture
Two Catholics not only accept but identify with the struggles of all
true artists, sensing the essentially religious nature of their labors,
recognizing that they expend the same spiritual energies that they
themselves do pursuing the mystery of daily life.

In the once terrible beauty of Culture One, the church seemed a glistening cloud-beribboned castle whose monarchs felt that they not only monopolized but had a right to monitor, judge, and control all religious experience. The institution claimed the exclusive world rights to holiness, grudgingly allowing that intense spiritual lives could be led outside its walls but only in extreme circumstances or according to instructive providential designs. Such non-Catholic religious persons were thereby invisibly tied to the official church, which arrogated jurisdiction over them to itself, conferring on them an honorary, and therefore controllable, Catholic identity through such notions as "anonymous" Christianity and "baptism of desire."

Currently, Culture Two Catholics understand that the official supervision and licensing of the spiritual life are as antithetical to its nature as to the nature of art itself. Ecclesiastical administrators cannot exercise control over what is, at heart, utterly human and mysterious. His papal sponsor may have nagged Michelangelo, lying flat on his scaffolding contemplating divine truths, but he could not enter into or shape his creative work or his spiritual vision. The Christian life is, in fact, a work of art, its dynamics exactly those familiar to every honest artist—the awesome dying and being born again that are the inner strength and spiritual source of authority for any true creation. The authority of genuine art is, therefore, non-manipulative and essentially simple; art speaks for itself. Great art, like a great life, addresses us in a unique voice; that is why we turn and give our attention to both of these, willingly obedient to their internal authority. They are versions of the quest for the grail, for that essentially spiritual mythic search, the pilgrimage, as in the myth of the Knights of King Arthur, always begun at the forest wall where no trail had yet been cut, in itself both poses the mystical question and answers it at the same time.

A holy life is a creative achievement that delivers the concentrated truth of an individual existence. Like the artist, the good person is aware of all that is "grave and constant," joyous and tragic, in the human landscape, and is committed to a transformation of the inner self, a passage through suffering and death to resurrection and a fuller experience of being alive. In the work of art and in holy lives we sense our own experience lived more intensely, lived, we might say, with authority. We respond willingly to good lives and good art, effortlessly acknowledging this authority. Again, this is not blind obedience to the will of another but a positive response to the evidence of our senses that nourishes and moves the imagination. Deep calls out to deep, health to health, and what the saint and the artist tell us of human experience deepens our understanding of our own. This critical exchange is healthy, for we emerge from it more alive than we were before it took place; every engagement with real holiness or genuine art is a resurrection.

The institutional church is true to its own organizational nature; it is only being itself when it attempts to control what is fundamentally beyond control—the natural, healthy instincts of good persons. One might say that the notion of perfection held by the organizational church has been a case of mistaken identity. Its administrators misidentified obsessive orderliness as holiness, consequently ruling out the moderate, common, and eminently tolerable disorder of imperfection that is the condition of any well-lived and healthy life. Health was ruled out on a technicality because it did not fit easily into any canonical category. But no one can write rules for healthy people. That is the burden of St. Paul's extraordinary reflections on the nature of love in First Corinthians. Love and health share the same simplicity of appearance, the same lack of manipulative intent. For centuries, however, healthy people were made to feel guilty because they could not lead unhealthy lives perfectly, while many neurotic people were rewarded because they could. The thought of all the generous, earnest efforts on the part of good people to subdue what was humanly healthy about themselves in order to fit the institutional model of sanctity retains a terrible power to break the heart.

Such good persons—seminarians and men and women candidates for the religious life—thought that their superiors knew what they were doing and submitted to their wishes, often with disastrous consequences for themselves. Those who survived these regimes, which forced a Cartesian dualism into their spiritual lives, did so because of their basic health. Similarly, married people made heroic efforts to comply with institutional expectations about their own conduct, frequently at a tragically high price to themselves and their families. Indeed, the darker aspects of the culture so dominated by the imperial institution became the theme of great exile Catholic artists. No writer more clearly explored the lonely, conflicted, and unsentimentalized world of the priesthood during that early century high point of clerical culture than J. F. Powers. It took such artists to examine and exorcise the demons of estrangement, loneliness, and heartbreak that entered so many people through this split spiritual vision of the human person. It is, therefore, not surprising that many people have now pulled back from automatically accepting the authority of those institutional churchmen who insist on the hierarchical ordering not only of the church but of the spiritual life as well. What healthy people sense about such self-appointed supervisors is their distance from the realities of human experience.

The institution's claim that the crown of holiness was granted to those who observed with exhausting exactitude myriad regulations led to demonic and debilitating ascetic competitions, many of which had a pathological underside, in which the tension arose from a basic, if unacknowledged, conflict between the individual and the organization. Individuals who kept the rules heroically, going beyond the institution's demands, won freedom, as we will see presently, from its supervisory power and, in many cases, such as those of the great medieval women saints, became a threat to it. For the moment, however, we may observe that goodness and health are not easily categorized and certainly cannot be subjected to domination by others without suffering serious loss or distortion. Culture Two Catholics have recaptured a basic Christian understanding of personality by embracing health as the most trustworthy sign of the spirit. This represents a return to the spiritual life as art rather than as law, and to metaphor rather than concrete discourse as religion's native language. This is the territory of the artist and the saint, human, ever mysterious and ambivalent, chartable only one step at a time. One thinks of St. John of the Cross's remark about the summit of perfection, "There is no way here." That matches exactly the instruction given the Arthurian knights as they departed on their quests; each was, as mentioned, to "enter the forest at its darkest part." There was, and is, no spiritual grail to be found at the end of a path hacked out by another. On any pilgrimage powerful enough to change us, we are on our own.

A holy life, like a poem, a painting, or a piece of sculpture, is, as its linguistic roots attest, something whole. The root of the word holy is *kailo,* which in old English became *hal,* or whole, as in *halsum,* or wholesome. Is it accidental that in French we come upon it as the sturdy support of the feminine name *Hel*oise? Or that *health, holy,* and *hallow* bloom from this same stem of language? Holiness is not to be associated with the denial of existence, the refusal to see or hear or eat, but with its affirmation and the good use of the senses. So Jesus says, in John, "I have come that they may have life, and life to the full." In a classic evocation of holiness, St. Irenaeus says that "the glory of God is a man fully alive."

The quest for holiness and the struggle for true art are intimately related efforts. Both seek to render human experience whole and intelligible. Holiness perceived fundamentally as a gradual extirpation of the earthy components of personality, a steady effort to purify the self of every claim of the body, represented an estrangement from the traditional understanding of holiness implicit in the church's central teaching of the Incarnation, in which God does not reject but "takes on the body of a man," accepting all human aches and joys, save sin, at the same time.

Institutional church leaders appear never to have observed the bright and revealing irony of their post-mortem appreciation of the body and sanctity. During life's arduous passage toward holiness the body was to be despised, maltreated in the name of spiritual perfection. At the moment of death the corpse, the flesh safe now from its familiar shudders, became sacred, an appraisal reinforced, peculiarly enough, if after death's visitation the body remained lifelike in appearance. Such a body was feasted on by its venerators, and relics of hair and bone, even articles of clothing or objects touched to the corpse, were thought to have curative powers, and, inserted as minute fragments into miniature, monstrance-like vessels, became important not only to the cult of the deceased but to the unabashed commercial enterprises that grew from them. Culture One, at its zenith, had an enormous inventory of blessed remains under its jurisdiction. Like seeds cast into the wind, these relics were found everywhere in the culture—at the shrines of the saints, in glinting reliquaries on thousands of mantelpieces, pinned on the swaddling clothes of infants and the bed linen of the dying. The institution was able to revere in death the body that it barely tolerated in life.

Culture Two Catholics have sensed the incongruity of notions of sanctity that celebrated the body only after rigor mortis had set in. This was, in effect, an institutional act of sacrilege against the teachings of Jesus and, indeed, against the most obvious meaning of his having "taken on the body of a man." The church, its profoundly human inclinations revived by the fresh waters of Vatican II theology, has renewed its incarnational self-understanding. In the conciliar documents, the church defines itself not as an institution but as mystery, a people of God, a mystery, then, of active human relationships that do not need death to validate their simple goodness. Culture Two Catholics no longer romanticize the ideal of sanctity split off from the pursuit of a full and honorable life in the compelling, mysterious unity of soul and body. The great battle of existence cannot pit these elements against each other; the struggle is to become whole, even imperfectly, rather than to endure a false division of the self. This striving for integrity resembles that of the artist and the effort is not only lighted from within by its own distinctive authority. So, too, it is intrinsically generative, shorn of meaning unless it gives and nourishes life. Sanctity, in the healthiest intuition of Culture Two, cannot be life denying or deliberately barren.

Many sincere Culture One Catholics still give strong evidence of their indoctrination during the golden age in which religion was partitioned off from life in general, so that it fell, in what seemed an almost natural way, under the aegis and control of the administrative church. Religion was not permitted far beyond this closely guarded area; Sunday was the day for faith, the interval in which to contemplate the supernatural plane that floated just beyond the reach of earthlings. Anything wholly "natural," such as a spontaneous response of love, could only be made worthy, that is "supernaturalized," through a mental transformation that invested the act with grace. Otherwise, despite the authority such responses bore because of their generosity or nobility, they were merely "natural," pagan distant cousins to institutionally validated examples of holiness. Culture One actively rejected the integration of faith into the other activities of life.

That careful distinction between the personal, spiritual life and the public, professional life allowed the development of the famous Catholic political and business consciences. Men felt that, if they fulfilled their institutional religious obligations, they were free to become friendly on their own terms with the mammon of iniquity during the rest of the week. Papal encyclicals on labor were not warmly welcomed by many Catholic businessmen, who felt that the church should mind its own spiritual preserves and stay out of theirs. If soul and body and spirit and flesh were divisible, so were these universes of concern. One of my most vivid encounters with that mentality occurred when I visited an old politician in a federal prison and he spent most of the time speaking of his pilgrimages to religious shrines and of his continuing habit of sleeping on his side to leave room for his guardian angel. In short, how to be a good Catholic while serving time for mail fraud and embezzlement.

This is the landscape poet T. S. Eliot once described as the "Waste Land," which, as Joseph Campbell has observed, is "a world in which . . . force and not love, indoctrination, not education, authority, not experience, prevail in the ordering of lives, and where the myths and rites enforced and received are consequently unrelated to the actual inward realizations, needs, and potentialities of those upon whom they are impressed."*

*The Masks of God: Creative Mythology, New York, Viking Press, 1968, p. 388.

"And we are here," as Matthew Arnold wrote of the same forsaken place, "as on a darkling plain / Swept with confused alarms of struggle and flight / Where ignorant armies clash by night."* The intuitively spiritual—mystics, artists, and healthy ordinary people—stand together, as they have throughout history, as the true counterculturists, who feel deep within themselves the falseness of the apparent triumphs of their times. This occurs whenever appearances are valued more than reality and are propped up by a combination of power and deceptive language. Such strategies betray the healthy and healing quest for truth—for authoritative truth, we might say—the search for the grail that is the calling of all creative and generative people. Throughout history, such persons have stood apart from the insistent, power-imbued culture, whether of church or state, to reject its hypocrisy, and, at that darkened mass of forest, to find their own path.

Indeed, the condition described by Eliot in his famous 1922 poem ("I Tiresias, though blind, throbbing between two lives...") was that, not only of our time, but of the world, as Campbell observes "torn between honor and love ... [that] was to be cured of its irresolution" through the experience described in the legend of the Holy Grail.† And, as rendered by Wolfram von Eschenbach, this story of Parzival is a tale of devastated Christianity—that is, a waste land of corrupted authority—"symbolically attributed to the awesome wounding of the young Grail King Anfortas ...This calamity ... was symbolic ... of the dissociation within Christendom of spirit from nature: the denial of nature as corrupt, the imposition of what was supposed to be authority *super*naturally endowed, and the actual demolishment of both nature and truth in consequence."‡ But, in order to grasp the dynamics of this legend, so clearly the same ones

---

*Dover Beach," stanza 4.
†Joseph Campbell, *Myths to Live By,* New York, Bantam edition, 1973, p. 166.
‡*Ibid.,* pp. 167, 168.

experienced by all who seek spiritual truth today, let Joseph Campbell tell us the rest of this story:

> The mystical law governing the adventure required that the
> hero to achieve it should have no knowledge of its task or
> rules, but accomplish all spontaneously on the impulse of his
> nature. . . . And the task then expected of him, when the
> maimed king on his litter would be carried into the stately hall,
> would be simply to ask what ailed him. The wound would
> immediately heal, the waste land would become green. . . .
> However, on the occasion of his first arrival and reception,
> Parzival, though moved to compassion, politely held his peace,
> for he had been taught . . . that a knight does not ask questions.
> Thus he allowed concern for his social image to inhibit the
> impulse of his nature—which, of course, was exactly what
> everyone else in the world was doing in that period and was
> the cause of all that was wrong.*

As a result, as those familiar with the story know, the young
misguided knight was exiled from the Grail realm and only as he
persisted, out of compassion for the wounded king, was he ultimately able to complete his task. The climax of the story follows a
battle with his elder Moslem half-brother, which led to their recognition of each other, "an allegorical reference to the two opposed
religions of the time, Christianity and Islam: 'two noble sons,' so to
say, 'of one father.' "† Both are invited to the castle, the king is
healed, and Parzival takes his place. The elements of this adventure
match those required in our own day for any who would heal the
division between the church as a powerful institution and as a People
of God, thereby making the waste land bloom: confidence in healthy
inner impulses, especially that of compassion, and a willingness to
recognize the relationship that transcends religious institutional

---

Ibid., p. 169.
†*Ibid.,* p. 170.

claims to exclusivity of redemptive franchise, between ourselves and all members of the human family.

The spiritual waste land of our own time will flourish, not in response to authoritarian assertions or the implementation of institutional force, but in response to the same profoundly spiritual realizations to which we must finally be obedient, that is, to whose whisperings we must listen and respond. All artists and believers are called to heal the wounded king, not through repeating formulas insisted on by others, but through the natural, healthy power of their own loving compassion for others.

The genuine artist and the good person are drawn, as the knights were toward the spiritual meaning of the grail, by an inner sense of direction to the healthy integration of life's elements; they actively seek wholeness. Their nonmanipulative commitment to this fullness of being in their lives and work attracts our freely bestowed attention. Although they do not insist on, or perhaps even think much about, their authority, it is theirs as ripeness belongs to the nature of the harvest and grandeur to the sunset spreading itself along the horizon; their authority is indisputable and irresistible and it has nothing to do with controlling other persons. It is easy to tell, in life and in art, when people know what they are doing. The authority of art is linked inseparably to the vision, intention, and skills of artists, no matter what their medium.

Artists take the pieces of life, the shards of good and bad, of love and friendship, of pain, tragedy, and misunderstanding that confront us all, and endow them with a wholeness that allows us to penetrate the mystery in which our lives are set. They heal our wounds with their compassionate perception and rendering of our striving and our falling short. In their work, they address our total personalities, both conscious and unconscious, leading us more deeply into ourselves, into the furthest recesses of our identity, supporting our stance on the ever-shifting ground of existence. Such persons do not strike the great tent of mystery that billows above us but rather allow us to see its intricate folds and webbing, the mysteries coiled within mystery in the great dwelling of life.

Artists make it possible for us to accept and deal with the magnificent, sometimes comforting, sometimes terrifying ambiguities of our experience. In similar fashion, good persons—holy people—pull together the same easily scattered human elements, not cheaply or superficially, but in the authentically generative fashion that flows from their being responsibly human instead of striking shallow angelic poses. These include shaping a consistent and serious moral vision, and a willingness to expose themselves to hurt—to the dangerous possibilities of failure and rejection—in their efforts to love. They are true seekers of the grail, entering the forest every day at its darkest part. The medium of holy persons is life, and, much like artists, they translate it steadily by respecting, perhaps in the painful act of always rediscovering, its ineffable mystery. They have authority not because they solve the mystery but because they understand that nobody ever can. The great German Jesuit theologian Karl Rahner once said that the mystery of the universe that frustrated Einstein was precisely what attracted him.

Religious persons, like artists, have no easy task in making something fresh, unique, and wondrous of these familiar, perennially perplexing materials of our human situation. That willingness to look again at life defines the nature of respect for life (respect, from *respicere,* means *to look again*) and the capacity for compassion. *Respect for Life,* a slogan much used by the institutional church in its campaigns of education against birth control and abortion, cannot be reduced to these few, albeit important, moral issues. Respect for life connotes a richer comprehension of the complex tasks of existence and of the special authority that individuals manifest through the unselfish love by which they impress a distinctive moral configuration on their lives. This authority is one with and inseparable from the healthy obligation of making something whole out of the diverse aspects of life itself. It is therefore totally different from the authoritarianism falsely invoked as authority by ecclesiastical bureaucrats. Genuine authority, as mentioned often, speaks directly to the human imagination and only indirectly to the will.

Confidence in healthy instincts and intuitions, friendliness to the inner self's striving for wholeness: these are concepts that were not readily accepted in the triumphant age of Culture One. It is not surprising to find that art, other than as the affirmation of institutionally acceptable themes, was looked on with enormous suspicion during that period. It was, indeed, a waste land, although its ecclesiastical proprietors seemed pleased with its severe and well-ordered bleakness. Barrenness was what they wanted. George N. Shuster, then editor of *Commonweal,* suggested in 1922, for example, that "the great bulk of American Catholic fiction is unintelligent and unreadable."

In a recent study of Catholic periodical fiction during that high age of Culture One (1930–1950), Joseph M. McShane observes the clear identification of many Catholic writers with institutional purposes. Their stories, for example, sharply criticized women seeking careers outside the home, warned of the dangers of mixed marriages, divorce, and birth control. As he notes,

> The destructive potential of the modern world was not exhausted by its threats against marriage and its temptations . . . the writers also warned . . . about the dangerous moral relativism and agnosticism that could result from any education beyond high school . . . or from pursuing professional careers in scientific or medical research. To counterbalance the corrosive influence of education, the readers were exhorted to lead lives marked by peasant or childlike faith. . . . Fear created a ghetto in which thought and creativity were devalued, and passivity encouraged.*

While certain redeeming pockets of concern for the artist existed in the shadowed nooks of Culture One, as in the Dominican Fathers' sponsorship of the theater, or in the literary interests of the Jesuits, novelists such as Harry Sylvester and J. F. Powers who bravely explored the psychological interior of Catholicism in the forties, swam against a powerful cultural stream, and won their literary recognition in the world at large rather than within Catholicism itself. Why this bleak reception for the artist, of whose calling the

*U.S. Catholic Historian, Vol. 6, Number 2/3, Spring/Summer 1987, pp. 188, 189.

church was once the greatest supporter, and in whose work, as in that of Michelangelo or Raphael, Catholic theology was once so gloriously expressed? The answer, in accord with dynamics to be explored in greater detail later, is found less in the church's concern for the purity of religious truth than in its anxiety to preserve and enhance the effective power of its organizational structures. Institutions suppress the natural response, so healthy and sacramentally significant in the account of Parzival's quest, Everyman's calling. The authority that a church possesses because of its sacramental insight is quickly dissipated when it chooses to follow its institutional reflexes instead of its healthiest instincts.

Artists, by nature, are antagonists of the institutionalization of existence, persons who cannot successfully fulfill their calling under the control of bureaucrats, however benign. The plight of Catholics with artistic souls was, therefore, extraordinarily frustrating and painful in the church until little more than a generation ago. Vatican II began to welcome them back just as it made possible the related development of Culture Two Catholicism. Only in this free environment were artists once again warmly invited, appreciated, and recognized as legitimate explorers of all human experience, who could, as novelists by their very title claim, return from their daily work with "something new" to tell us about its mountains and hidden valleys. That is the grail found and brought back to us by serious artists of every kind.

Culture Two, in part because its members were given rich opportunities for higher education by Culture One, has had the leisure as well as the perspective to appreciate the intimate kinship of art and religion. It was Culture One, as we have noted, that made Vatican II possible, and, within it, put an end to the *Index* of prohibited books that had so tightly controlled Catholics' freedom to read. In this new and congenial atmosphere, art, like a cathedral freed from the grip of massive scaffolding, shoulders its majestic lines in the sunlight and speaks its silent spiritual language across the landscape. Culture Two makes room for artists to pursue their own inner visions. It is impossible to be against art and for religion, unless one or the other is so falsified as to be unrecognizable. That is why the present tension within Catholicism has come to center on the nature of religion itself. That is a waste-land dilemma. The institutionalists perceive religion as a literal, non-artistic, tightly controllable phenomenon. In short, a mirror held far away and at a distorting angle from reality. Catholics not consumed by institutional concerns understand religion as something far different, something timeless beneath the accidents of time, the mysterious that streams from the vents of everyday experience, rich and dappled, sacramental and inexhaustible, bearing as the air bears light every human mood and rhythm.

In his quest for the grail the poet Thomas Merton not only relived the dynamic elements of challenge in the lives of the knights and of monks like Abelard who preceded him, but he worked out a destiny (*wyrd,* that active pursuit of an unfolding fate, as it is called in the classical legends) similar to that of every Culture Two Catholic. It was almost exactly that of many creative, truly spiritual artists (in the broadest sense) who gave themselves to an institutional church that had lost touch with its own poetic strengths. With the best of intentions, the administrative church did not know what to do with him and, puzzled by his creative yearnings and restlessness, attempted to control rather than encourage him in a variety of ways throughout his life. As a Trappist, he became celebrated for his autobiography, *The Seven Storey Mountain,* the narrative of his movement out of his literary Columbia University milieu into the stark calling of the ever-silent monk. It was a pilgrimage that matched perfectly the highly romantic aspects of Culture One's postwar glory.

So far, so good. The real story, brilliantly revealed in Michael Mott's biography, was far different.* Merton the monk lost the freedom to follow his own inner intuitions. He was forced, under obedience, to write explicitly "religious" books, lives of Trappist saints and other works that reinforced the institution and helped greatly to support his monastery. His works were censored by men who did not comprehend them, his desire to live part of the time in

---

The Seven Mountains of Thomas Merton, Boston, Houghton Mifflin, 1984.

a hermitage was represented to Roman authorities by his own abbot as the request of "an emotional, unstable sort of person who was trying to avoid living a normal life."* He was even accused by a leading Catholic psychoanalyst, Gregory Zilboorg, of being, among other things, "a gadfly . . . very stubborn . . . megalomania and narcissism are your big trends."†

Yet Merton the monk could not overcome Merton the artist, and he gradually made a separate, uneasy peace with the Trappists, moving out of the community into a cabin of his own, as, indeed, Abelard had centuries before him. Merton also moved in many ways back into the world, stumbling, as an artist in such a situation must, making his way out as he wrote again on the subjects that were his own, forging a new extra-institutional life and identity that were in part clumsy, in part poignant, and immensely human. Mott's biography is clearly an account of Merton's search for the grail, that ultimate symbol of spiritual meaning.

Merton was, one might surmise against the overspiritualized Culture One interpretations of his life, making his way by trial and error out of that culture, not wanting to hurt anyone but needing to get out, seeking health according to the authority of his internal sense of balance. His inner sensitivity made him aware of the universality of the religious impulse as well as of contemplation as its rich common thread. So he wrote, as he gradually moved deeper into an appreciation of the bonds between all the great religious traditions, that for him "Catholicism is not confined to one culture, one nation, one age, and one race . . . my Catholicism is all the world and all the ages."‡ And, if he lamented the crisis that monasticism itself was enduring in a time of renewal, Merton was also searching for some different setting in which to live out his own life and a deeper language in which to sing of it.

Consider Abelard near the end of his life. Half a man, having been castrated by Heloise's uncles, celebrated as an exiled philosopher

*Ibid., p. 338.
†Ibid., p. 295.
‡Ibid., p. 315.

and poet, finding an audience outside the church rather than in its administrators, he was, as Campbell observes,

> harried from pillar to post for his views, driven throughout his mutilated life from one monastic haven to another. On one occasion he was compelled to burn his own book with his own hands ("So it was burnt," he wrote of this brutal event, "amid general silence"); and to read aloud then the Athanasian Creed ("the which I read amid sobs and tears as well as I might"). He was sent to a convent near Soissons, which had acquired the reputation of a penitentiary . . . only to fall into more trouble, and then more, until at one point he fled to a forest hermitage, to which . . . students flocked. . . . "God knows," he wrote of those terrible years, "that at times I fell into such despair that I proposed to myself to go off and live the life of a Christian among the enemies of Christ."*

So, Merton, near the end of his life, vexed and on the move, finding even his hermitage filled with guests, a celebrity corresponding with the great writers and spiritual thinkers of his time, but a man under suspicion by his superiors for what they could only perceive as his highly irregular activities. In his last, extraordinarily restless years Merton fell in love with a young nurse, involved himself in clandestine meetings, phone calls from the monastery that were overheard, a consuming relationship, which, like Abelard, he finally abandoned for the monastery. He seemed to resolve the relationship, but he did call the nurse, identified by Merton's biographer only as S., for a last time in the year he died, saying, "We are two half people wandering in two lost worlds."† He became a pilgrim again, seeking something that even as an artist he was not able fully to name. While pursuing an understanding of the limits of contemplation in the Far East, he died, either from a heart attack or through electrocution by a faulty fan cord. His death remains mysterious in a poetically, sacramentally

---

*The Masks of God, p. 397.
†Mott, p. 454.

appropriate way a generation after its occurrence. In his final talk, Merton seemed to hint about his long, lonely journey's end, speaking clearly from his unconscious to his colleagues as the morning concluded, "so I will disappear from view . . ."

His biographer observes that "in his journals Merton had talked over and over of disappearing."* Merton's life may be viewed as something composed by the poet within, a true rendering of the contemporary spiritual voyager, who came to feel trapped in the administrative church that had once seemed his romantic salvation, the artist who suffered, in advance as poets always do, what millions of his fellow Catholics would experience in the generation after his death. Perhaps it is not too far off the mark to say of him, as Campbell did of Abelard, that he "was indeed Tristan as the mutilated Grail King, and he stands symbolic for his time and for the sterilization of heart, body, and mind that the Waste Land theme represents."†

Merton's life was thus the model for legions of creative people who baffled the institution and who paid high prices for being originals who did not fit easily into precut placements. Some suffered enormously, yielding up their untapped creativity to the unresponsive but hugely confident, and, one might add, generally benevolent, if smugly so, institution of Catholicism. Others experienced severe problems in trying to adjust to lives in which they could never feel comfortable or fulfilled. They all bear the wounds of the Grail King known to Abelard and Merton as well, for the administrative church emasculated them in its efforts to control them. Thus, authoritarian instincts to this day, in the name of a pure teaching authority, heap shame on the sexual dimensions of human personality.

Many highly creative persons in the clergy and religious life, as we have discussed, gradually moved out of its central core, toward marginal lives in which, like Merton, they fashioned a ledge just broad enough to stand on outside the massive walls, a perilous purchase of freedom that the organization did not know how to give

*Ibid., p. 564.
†The Masks of God., p. 397.

them directly. And, for all the struggle and disorder of his long journey, one might ask who now possesses true spiritual authority, Thomas Merton or a generation and more of nameless ecclesiastical bureaucrats who shook their heads at him? Who touches and opens our hearts, Merton or the monk who criticized him to Roman authority for not wanting to live a "normal life"?

Mystery thrives in the lives of the knowing and the loving. Its metaphors are everywhere in the scriptures, as in the psalmist's images of the wondrous creatures of nature, of nestlings under the protective wings of greater birds, of harts panting for living water. In short, the Bible presents mystery loose in the universe, mystery everywhere for those with eyes to see and ears to hear, mystery in the very texture of life, mystery the discernible aura around every truly human event. Joseph Cardinal Ratzinger, now head of the Congregation for the Doctrine of the Faith, has lamented the loss of mystery in Roman Catholicism. As a sensitive and well-trained theologian, Ratzinger may have felt the enormous pressures that a creative person experiences when he must give himself to administrative tasks. He may, in fact, be experiencing mystery deprivation in an office that requires him to control rather than engage in speculative theology. Perhaps in this man, so often perceived as the symbol of the institution, we have a new yet classic example of the creative person surrendering everything for the sake of the institution. Perhaps there is more Merton in him than he knows. He may not even realize that when he speaks of the absence of mystery in contemporary Catholicism he is revealing the depth of his own loss. Cardinal Ratzinger may himself bear wounds that he has not yet realized to be those of the legend of the grail seeker first written down in his own homeland a thousand years ago by von Eschenbach.

Only those with a lively feeling for mystery can grasp the correspondence between the creative process and the essential dynamics of the central Catholic understanding about life. For if we are all caught up in the search for the spiritual grail, we can recognize that the redemptive pattern of life, death, and resurrection is as common in ordinary life as it is, in intensified form, in the work of the artist. This cadenced experience of yielding up the self, that is, passing through death in order to achieve a deeper and fuller life, lies just below the surface of daily existence; its outlines can be found in every human transaction that has any genuine weight or meaning. This sequence is commonplace for spouses and parents, for teachers and pastors, for friends and lovers everywhere. Nothing reveals the identification of art and religion in a more telling manner than a comparison of the creative process with life itself.

Creative artists, whose long line started well before Abelard and continues beyond Merton, are concerned with a vision of the possible. They are, therefore, essentially persons of faith, for they are ever committed to a world that longs to come into being. Religious faith is of the same grain and texture as the faith that couples have in each other, in their families, and in their communities. The act of bringing the possible into existence defines the generative dimension of the authority that we have already explored in detail. What does the nature of the creative artistic process tell us about the generative authority that marks the lives of Culture Two Catholics?

Poets, in the studies of creative persons carried out by psychologist Frank Barron, speak of learning to "throw themselves away," of having to surrender themselves in pursuit of their art. They experience a certain disorganization of their adjustment in order to achieve the new and higher level of integration, the "wholeness" they express in their work. Barron described this as an experience of "diffusion," a breaching of their ego boundaries in order to bring them together again in the fulfillment of poetic achievement. Barron gives the following description of the creative artist's experience:

. . . the individual is willing to "die unto himself," i.e., to permit an achieved adaptation or state of relative equilibrium to perish. And there are not guarantees that something better will thereby be arrived at. Looking backwards from the end point of the creative process, we are inclined to say, "Ah, yes, it had to be so; the chance had to be taken; the chalice could not be passed; the agony was necessary for the redemption and the resurrection." But facing forward in time we see only risk and difficulty, and if we have not the courage to endure diffusion ("suffer death") we cannot achieve the new and more inclusive integration ("gain the light").*

Works of art that emerge from such a process have the power to speak authoritatively to us; we recognize what we term, in a related word, the authenticity of the work. That always comes from within. The papers and documents of appraisers and art experts do not confer it. When these are reliable, they merely affirm what the work of art possesses in and of itself. So, too, the lives of good people—those who truly enlarge others through their relationships—have an internal strength purchased at the price of embracing the redemptive sequence of death and resurrection. This is the spiritual authority, so enlivening of the imagination, recognized and responded to by Culture Two Catholicism.

It may have been with just such a sense of the relationship between the authority of true art and true religion that Pope Paul VI resisted the advice he had received to sell off the contents of the Vatican Museum. Instead, he refurbished it, opening a wing for modern art in the area immediately adjacent to the Sistine Chapel. This profound gesture signified a fresh acceptance of the genuine artist as an honored citizen of the Kingdom. Paul VI spoke, at the wing's dedication, of the need for the prophetic voice of the artist to be heard in the heart of the Vatican. In an era marked by institutional rebuilding and reform, Paul fashioned a sign in the fashion of a genuine artist, against the grain of his counselors. So Paul spoke for all the seekers of the spiritual grail, honoring all those who, like legions of Abelards and Mertons, have suffered pursuing the kingdom of God within them. Paul's gesture may one day be understood for what it was, a great act of faith in a church that was coming into being, a church that is more a servant people and less of a dominating institution, a healer of the wounded rather than a wounder of the healers.

*"Diffusion, Integration, and Enduring Attention," in *Study of Lives,* ed. by Robert W. White (New York: Prentice-Hall, 1963), p. 247.

13

The *Titanic* and the *Challenger*

Authority and Faith

He that has ears to hear, let him hear.

—Matthew 11:15

The terms which, in his inmost heart, each man knows. As I know mine. As all know. For that is the truth of it—that we all know, God, that we know, that we know, we know, we know.

—Saul Bellow, *Mr. Sammler's Planet*

The authority of religion, like that of art, flows from internal rather than external sources. Institutions, such as the church, do not confer authority on religion anymore than museums do on works of art. The best they can do is to recognize the authority that these phenomena possess and to provide a setting that does not overwhelm what it is meant to underscore. This is increasingly difficult to understand in a culture in which so many self-appointed authorities, and their peculiar, perhaps demonic instrumentation, intervene between individuals and works of art. When we depend excessively on someone else's voice not only to identify but to interpret acceptable art, we risk never hearing the artists speak directly to us in their own special language. The role of intermediaries, in art or religion, is not to overshadow the work or to usurp the voice of the artist, but to make sure that the conditions are right for our encounter with the creator and the Creator. This demands, among other things, that external authorities understand and accept the fact that they are not artists and do not possess artistic gifts. Often they are not even qualified to be critics. In their position as guardians and stewards, institutional managers might take the advice that Diogenes gave to the man who asked how he might help him: "Stand out of my light."

If the museum, the recital hall, the reading lamp, or the chapel— or the commentators or exegetes—draw more attention to themselves than to the art or spiritual mystery for which they exist, they fail utterly. If their intervention blocks us from a direct relationship to Picasso or Beethoven in their art, we remain untroubled by the demands of such encounters. Is Beethoven alive or dead when we listen to his music? It is a fine, unsettling question, one that should send tremors of uncertainty through us and set us wondering about time and timelessness. We need not answer the question finally, but we grow in some immeasurable way for letting it disturb us. But we will never even hear the question if an interposed voice whispers directions in our ear at the same time. This is an aspect of the domestication of creativity, determinedly doing good and thereby doing incidental ill, for art, artists, and the public. Art is always endangered when its protectors place their authority—their interpretation—disproportionately between creative workers and their audiences, or between God and believers.

Even artists cannot explain their work rationally; they can only shrug, referring us back to the medium in which they have already spoken in as disciplined and skillful a way as they can. Picasso once dismissed a curious onlooker by saying, "Don't talk to the driver." Any painter, musician, or writer who explains the work before or after is no true artist. The artist, as Pope John XXIII told the bishops at the beginning of Vatican II, finds his answers in doing the work at hand. The way of art is mysterious and the place to which it finally leads us is unpredictable. Religion cannot be less supple and mysterious or it would be unworthy of divine or human experience. Thus, the goal of a fully rationalized faith, each step fully illuminated, its final end fully and accurately perceived and defined, is contradictory and impossible.

The defense of any controlled education in the arts or theology is that it makes them more accessible and understandable to the public at large. The specter of the Enlightenment grins over the shoulder of the lecturer or liturgist who claims to be making the painting or the Mass more reasonable to viewers or worshipers. Nothing genuinely artistic—and nothing genuinely religious—is reasonable in the well-ordered, categorizable sense in which we use that term. Life, in fact, is not rational; nothing truly human ever is. Hence our need for art and religion, for openings on experience that enable us to confront and deal with the unreasonable, the ambiguous, and the mysterious, the inescapable elements of our existence. A faith completely under the control of its administrators, one that is defined solely in terms of intellectual statements uttered in one language in one historical period, speaks hoarsely, if at all, garroted by its own manipulators. Such faith may sound well ordered, or highly rational, but that is no accomplishment in a realm of experience whose internal logic is not that of the bureaucrat but of the poet. Neither faith, art, or the deepest experience of ordinary life, such as love, can submit to external control and survive.

Translating the Mass into English, as we have noted, was a triumph for those who felt that the Eucharist should be a reasonable experience. This change, heralded as an advance, paid insufficient attention to the internal authority of the Eucharist that, as a rite of mystery, speaks to the levels of personality that are inaccessible to reason or logic. The power of the Mass has survived liturgical adaptation and is an excellent example of religious symbolism whose authority—whose capacity to make us attend to it—comes from within itself rather than from those who comment on or explain it. Religion is not meant to be a controlled substance; it is as dangerous as great art because it speaks directly to our whole selves. We need not understand it—anymore than we need to understand human hope or love—to have it work its effects on us. And, as it is a perilous thing to fall into the hands of the living God, so also it is dangerous to encounter untamed mystery. The danger arises from the light that pours from it into our own inner selves.

Culture Two Catholics understand that religion cannot be totally domesticated or controlled. They perceive the institutional church as the guardian of the mysteries of faith but not their author and certainly not their master. The deepest authority of the church is rooted in the internal character of faith, in a profound sacramental grasp of human experience, not from institutional, administrative claims made by leaders who do not understand or easily speak its metaphorical spiritual language.

As the 1987 pilgrimage of Pope John Paul II began, a rather successful campaign to blame Culture Two Catholics for problems within the church was initiated. They were charged, as already observed, with being "cafeteria" or "selective" Catholics. Much was made of a rigorous, literal interpretation of the church's dogmatic and moral positions, with the intimation that those who dissented from any of these were exiling themselves from the fold of true believers. Indeed, the pope himself, addressing the American bishops in Los Angeles, said that such a questioning stance was "totally incompatible with being a Catholic." The burden was thus placed on Catholics, especially of the second culture, to justify, if not to repent, their positions to the church assembled. Indeed, the church was described by Pope John Paul II as a vertical rather than horizontal reality, a *communio* of hierarchical character rather than a People of God in collegial relationship with each other.

The integrity of the institution's self-assured hierarchical position was thus taken for granted. In this delicate area, replete with so many implications for ecclesiastical authority, scant attention was paid to the true tradition of Catholic teaching on dogmatic and moral issues. Nothing, as a matter of fact, is more traditional or compatible with Catholicism than the freedom to approach teachings from a variety of directions. Now dusty pre–Vatican II dogmatic textbooks include theological notes on the strength of belief expected or tolerated on various points or statements. Even in what are perceived by conservatives as the wonderful days of uniform belief in the church, subtle distinctions were made constantly about the grade of certitude associated with various teachings. Dogma was not as dogmatic as nostalgic Catholics would like to believe.

The same situation existed in moral theology. Catholics were free in their consciences to follow what were termed "probable opinions." These represented differing interpretations by individual theologians, or schools of theologians, of moral teachings on issues as widely different as the commandments. All moral theologians agreed on the primacy of conscience, that Catholics *were bound to follow their consciences* when they had formed them with deliberation and prayer, and they were to do this even if their judgments led them to act against some explicit Catholic teaching. The quality of probability attached to various teachings also varied; opinions could be *probable, more probable,* or *most probable,* and Catholics were free to follow any one of them as long, as the saying went, as they were "solidly probable." Human judgment obviously played a great role in these matters. This toleration, even encouragement, of diversity is as traditional as anything else in Roman Catholicism.

The mystery of ambiguity clings to everything, even to those elements that seem to be the most stable and conservative in Catholicism. Does not mystery haunt the majestic risings and fallings of Gregorian chant? The *Dies Irae* of the old church holds the sorrow of all the world's mourning, of its deeply known sadness, and, even as a memory, penetrates to the innermost marrow of personality. The heavily sentimentalized Jesus of so many devotional manuals can be cleansed, as treasures of art are, and he emerges again as a powerful presence. Even a devotion, such as that to the Sacred Heart of Jesus based on promises supposedly made to Saint Margaret Mary, can startle those who regard it as a classic example of Culture One antiquities. The second promise, "I will establish peace in their houses," almost aches with forgotten and contemporary strife, with all the unnamed suffering that has taken place inside family walls, bending time itself with their burden. We pause, for this out-of-date devotion for simple souls carries hints of unexpected complexity. The old Catholic adage of "offering up" suffering bears up well for anyone who understands that energy, even of the spiritual kind, is never lost but can be transformed and applied to other uses. It is by no means out of synchronization with our own times. Culture One, then, might examine its own resources before adopting the extirpation of ambiguity as a first principle of religious reform and theological discipline.

Ambiguity and pluralism deserve respect, for they constitute the atmosphere of the sacred spaces of life. Within this fragile envelope, much like that sustaining life on earth, mystery thrives and creative spiritual and pastoral services flourish. Studies of creative artists reveal that they are able to tolerate contradictory feelings, that they can live with opposite sentiments during that long period in which they are working out some way of resolving or harmonizing them in their work. The tension of standing at the convergence of swirling currents of emotion, perception, or conviction is a necessary condition for their working through the redemptive-like process of their art. The institutional church's inability to live with pluralism and ambiguity explains its suspicions of art and its estrangement from its own humanistic heritage. Uncomfortable with the fundamental conditions of creativity, it must insist on numbed and numbing conformity, on a static environment in which nothing new can be generated philosophically, scientifically, theologically, or spiritually. This, as we have seen, is the Waste Land.

As theologian Avery Dulles recently observed in an imagined statement to the pope:

> The church is perceived . . . scarcely as an inspirer of wisdom and creativity. Contemporary art and literature owe little to Christian faith, and Catholic philosophy—if the term is permitted at all—is in disarray. Theologians find themselves caught up in legalistic battles about the binding force of this or that doctrine. Few are boldly addressing the new problems presented by modern civilization, or lack of civilization. The kind

of critical mediation once accomplished by Clement and Origen, Augustine and Aquinas is scarcely being attempted any longer.*

In short, the institutional church has become so absorbed in preserving itself as a structure that it cannot grasp how it is destroying itself as a church. The deadly void born out of demands for such conformity is not a host environment for life or for vital religious faith. Institutions that disown or attempt to control metaphor evince a failure to comprehend or to speak the language of the Spirit. Metaphor comes from words that mean *to take across boundaries.* Through metaphors we are able to make journeys that are otherwise impossible for us. These are journeys incredibly complex and ambiguous for which no spiritual auto club can issue exact routings in advance. To insist on every article of faith as embodying a literal truth, as institutional Culture One administrators now do, is to destroy the mystical, religious meaning of this special language. In the long run, this diminishes the claims to authority that such institutional leaders make. It is evident that Culture Two Catholics have a better sense of metaphor and a deeper appreciation of the essential ambiguity and pluralism of life than many blaming Roman leaders do. It is hardly surprising that such Catholics would not obey, in the sense of listen to, such figures.

Mystery comes from the Greek *muein,* meaning to close, as the lips or the eyes, and signifies, according to the American Heritage Dictionary, "any belief in the existence of realities beyond perceptual or intellectual apprehension but directly accessible by intuition." In Latin, it derives from *intueri,* which means *to look at* or *to contemplate.* An institution cannot safely act as the guardian of mysteries if it has forgotten how to contemplate them or if it believes that they can be preserved, like biological specimens, in an eternal fixative. As Gary McEoin perceptively noted in connection with the 1987 papal American visit the contrasts between static faith and dynamic faith:

"If I Had Five Minutes with the Pope . . ." America, September 19, 1987, p. 126.

Some claimed that the Council had successfully adapted to the modern world and that consequently the process of adaptation should cease as is the view of Pope John Paul II and his advisers. . . . Its dynamic and eternal nature is described in a metaphor used by Pope John XXIII: The boat of Peter was not moving from one safe anchorage to another. It was launching out to unchartered seas to accompany the world on a voyage of discovery which would continue where humankind carried the created condition to the perfection intended by the Creator.*

To put this another way, church authorities need to exhibit spiritual insight more than managerial skills or aphoristic piety if they are to be credible at all. Yet, strangely enough, many Culture One leaders, as in their discomfort with the mytho-poetic language of faith, seem ill at ease with spontaneous challenges to reflect spiritually on the broken world that is their collective parish. Research on American bishops carried out under the direction of Dr. Frank J. Kobler at Loyola University of Chicago supports the observation that most bishops would rather answer their mail than meditate. They perform out of duty more than out of any natural creative sympathy for spiritual themes. They may, in this regard, match St. Peter, who protested that he did not understand spiritual things as Jesus made him head of his church. In any case, the bishops' religious authority—and that of the Roman Culture One—may increasingly depend on their inner spiritual resources rather than on their extrinsic claims to our attention in religious matters.

As such, they would be no different from any other believers who must come to terms with the nature of religious faith. Our capacity to believe develops through positive and negative experiences, and gradually assumes a discernible character. What is significant about faith, according to keen observers and researchers, is that its normal trajectory of growth arches from dependence on external authority to independent responsibility for its nature and content. The locus

*Catholic Herald, London, September 25, 1987, p. 2.

of authority necessarily shifts away from accepting a religious interpretation because it is given to us by our parents or teachers to examining it for ourselves and testing it against our own life experience. If we put aside the immature shell, we keep the meat that it held, valuing it in a new way and believing in it on our own authority. Healthy religious development demands increasing autonomy, a reshaping and reintegration of one's religious understandings and commitments, so that they are no longer held with the innocent dependent confidence of a child but with the scarred independence of hard-bought wisdom.

This process has been analyzed in various ways. Perhaps the most enduring and heuristic of these was developed by Gordon Allport, who distinguished two types of faith, intrinsic and extrinsic. By the latter, he referred to belief that was inherited along with other family or cultural characteristics and was accepted into adulthood without much questioning. Allport described the extrinsic believer as the person who uses faith to promote self-interest. For such individuals faith is like a garment to be put on in bad weather or on occasions when it will enhance one's position or image. Some call this an instrumental use of religion and identify it, for example, in the lives of certain politicians, who draw on it to help their election and then ignore any demands that faith may make on them. For these persons, religion can be compartmentalized, reserved for Sundays or special occasions. It is a faith that does not question and is not questioned. As such, it gives final, literal, and unambiguous answers about God and life. This is a nonintegrated form of religious belief.

Far different is the notion of intrinsic faith, in which religion becomes what Allport termed a "master motive" in life, through which individuals integrate and give meaning to their complex experiences. This faith is the outcome of a period of testing and exploration of the original, inherited family faith. Persons test their faith against their experience of a contradictory and broken world and, putting away the childish, dependent aspects of it, accept it on their own authority. It thus becomes a vital, inner organizing force that does not give final answers but rather prompts persons to ask deeper and more searching questions. Doubt and wonder are not incompatible with this mature religious orientation.

Almost two generations of research have refined Allport's initial concepts considerably and they are still the subject of much discussion. It is sufficient for our purposes to observe that, just as in any other sphere of life, human beings must gradually take responsibility for their own beliefs. While they must and will listen to genuine authority in this regard, the final responsibility for the configuration of their religious and moral lives is their own. They cannot blame or credit sources outside themselves for the kind of spiritual transformations they must work inside themselves. In the terms we have been using, they must be able to relinquish the *concrete* metaphors that they accepted in childhood as true representations of the world, and, by grasping the *spiritual* meaning of the same metaphor, successfully make passage across the boundary to an adult faith. This pilgrimage is, as some researchers have described intrinsic faith, an active quest in the darkness, more akin to the search for the grail in the Arthurian legends than to a bland, unquestioning acceptance of an unearned inheritance.

Far from being an easily entered refuge from the stern disciplinary demands of Culture One, Culture Two is entered, as great art is achieved, through facing and enduring multiplied tests of human suffering. Spiritual maturity is the best measure we have of the true believer and the real artist. Catholics enter Culture Two seeking spiritual strength to accept and make something constructive out of the inexorable pain of being. They trust their own spiritual intuitions as resonating well with the Christian tradition that appreciates the redemptive nature of suffering. Their lives have transparent authority, for it is not hard to see into the souls of genuinely good persons. Claims to religious authority made by Culture One leaders will be readily accepted if they reflect similar spiritual depth in their own lives and actions. If these administrators hold up a spiritual map, its patterns must match those of the fire-tried experience of their people.

Convincing authority in faith and art depends not on extrinsic endorsements but on inner wholeness and depth of spiritual vision. In short, the foundations of spiritual authority must be sunk into the bedrock of the soul. It is not difficult to tell the spiritual poseur from the person of authoritative spirituality. While the intense hunger for meaning may make some persons vulnerable to the manipulation of charlatan-like religious leaders, such as the more outrageous television evangelists or faddish gurus, there is no mistaking men and women of spiritual depth. They arrest our attention, often make us uneasy, seem to see into or speak directly to our innermost being. There is a big difference between the impact on one's soul of former evangelist Pat Robertson and that of Russian novelist Alexander Solzhenitsyn. Robertson's hearty earnestness telegraphs the sincere superficiality that makes him resemble a salesman rather than a spiritual leader. Solzhenitsyn sets the teeth on edge, hints at the dread one must face in order to forge spiritual convictions, unmistakably touches the spirit. There is no doubt about the inner sources of his spiritual authority. But you could also contrast Shirley MacLaine with Mother Teresa, or William F. Buckley, Jr., the pope's great critic, with Pope John XXIII and notice similar reactions.

The test of their spiritual authority is not whether church leaders can explain the deliberations of various church councils or elucidate the intellectual content of doctrine, but whether they demonstrate any understanding of the way people actually live. A sympathy for the human condition, a readiness to forgive and encourage sinners, a sacramental feeling for the significant junctures of growth, significant relationships, and loss in people's lives: these constitute the elements of spiritual awareness that possesses intrinsic and easily recognizable religious authority. Such attributes define the sacramental sense of the world that must inform and innervate the sacramental ministry of bishops and clergy.

Centuries ago, largely because of abuses in the personal lives of priests, it was decreed that the sacraments had their effects irrespective of the spiritual state of their ministers. But is that really so? Could something so humanly expressive be immune to the human expressing it? Communicated unlovingly or indifferently, the sacraments become automatic and mechanical gestures, easy to caricature as superstition or magic. The authority of pastoral ministers depends on their ability to give of themselves as they absolve, anoint, or feed persons with the Eucharist. Indeed, it is not as scowling inspectors of orthodoxy but as true sacramentally imbued pastors that Culture One leaders make themselves welcome in Culture Two and keep it in a warm and affectionate union with the institutional church.

We encounter here a curious paradox, for many churchmen who want to reestablish their authority over Culture Two Catholicism are not at ease with this essentially compassionate sacramental spiritual approach. The American bishops, for example, are at their best when they can speak in this unmistakable pastoral tone to their people. They are, however, more at ease reflecting on nuclear deterrence and economic issues than they are in meditating publicly on the human aspirations and sorrows of their flocks. It is little wonder that serious Catholics make up their own minds about crucial moral questions; they do not have confidence that institutional officials have any depth in understanding the internal realities of their daily existence.

There are wonderful exceptions, as, for example, New York's John Cardinal O'Connor, who carries out many pastoral missions, such as visiting AIDS patients regularly with little fanfare or publicity. So, too, Archbishop James Hickey of Washington, D.C., buried a well-known priest who had died of AIDS, transforming this tragedy into a sacramentally vivid occasion. The same tone was found in the reactions of men like Chicago's Joseph Cardinal Bernardin and Milwaukee's Archbishop Rembert Weakland to Pope John Paul II's raising, during his 1987 visit to America, the question of denying the sacraments to divorced Catholics. They, and other bishops, responded as gentle pastors would, with an appreciation for the rights of individual conscience, which they would not violate or challenge. Too often, however, the bishops at their sacramental best must be caught in a seemingly unofficial moment, they must be overheard to be heard at all.

Some Culture One leaders are too institutionalized, too commit-

ted to organizational ends, too wrapped up in dutiful piety to display
the pastoral spirituality that would marvelously refurbish their credibility. Let us examine a recent incident, a painful public experience
of loss in which we were all involved, an occasion that cried out for
the consolation of spiritual insight. Yet almost every Culture One
spokesperson who commented did so in institutional clichés reminis-
cent of the phrases hurriedly whispered into the bereaved one's ears
at a wake. This inability to respond spontaneously in other than
formal religious terms reflects the deadening quality of Culture
One's institutional insulation. It explains why so many of its leaders
have trouble maintaining their authority.

Just as in 1912 the *Titanic* sank in the old mythological field, so
in 1986 the *Challenger* shuttle exploded in the new mythological
environment of space. These extraordinary incidents bracket the
century, symbolizing the mystery of the still unfinished passage the
human race is making from one age into another. This is our quest
for the grail and we stand together ever at the darkest part of the
forest.

The rational problems connected with these losses are minor com-
pared to their spiritual significance. Just as the journey of the privileged and the poor on the great ocean vessel reflected the
hierarchical age then ending, so the lift-off of the astronauts—a
black, an Oriental, two women, and even a man named Smith—
caught the theme of cooperative interdependence just beginning.
The aura of the sacred surrounds these tragic incidents and we
cannot and will not put them out of our minds and souls. Yet hardly
any official church leader from Culture One has been able to speak
of the spiritual meaning of the shuttle's disintegration in space.
Although sorrowful and sympathetic in a kind and official way, they
seemed to have little capacity to do the one thing that would fulfill
their mission and strengthen their authority, that is, to catch and
reflect publicly and pastorally on the spiritual significance of the
awful event.

Americans well beyond the ranks of Culture Two Catholics search
the horizon constantly for those who can give them some sense of

meaning about their lives. That is what they were looking for on that bitter cold January morning in the apocalyptic imagery of plumed smoke and flame. Only a pseudo-explanation will come out of the scientific analysis and measurement of the debris that rained down into the depths of the sea. It may trace failures in the structures and decisions, blame may finally be placed on some individuals. This will not touch the mystery of that terrible morning anymore than did the cliché-like comments that poured out of politicians and preachers alike after the accident. Perhaps the porpoises who broke the water just as a memorial wreath fluttered down onto the Atlantic had a deeper consciousness of its being a mystery beyond words, perhaps deep cried out to deep to call forth the kind of symbol that matched its tragic grandeur.

We will never quite get over that explosion because, in fact, it addressed depths of ourselves we have learned to ignore or to drown out with distraction. The event was cosmic in nature, symbolic of yearnings seeded long ago in the human race. The shuttle symbolized our common destiny to live in the stars, to understand the universe as our home. It was on a pilgrimage to our future and we all sat in its cabin in some part of our imagination. The loss of the shuttle was a powerful mystery because it so intimately involved us as explorers not only of outer space but also of that inner space of ourselves as unified human beings. It wore the hard armor of rocketry but its essential nature was spiritual. We have suffered because not even our most prominent religious leaders speak easily of genuinely spiritual matters. They often seem like outsiders to what is inside each of us.

The resurgence of fundamentalist religion may have occurred because it offers such simple answers to mysteries that are truly cosmic. Other religious traditions have forgotten how to listen to or speak of them at all. Still, the contents of every remembered mystery were there. Its elements were basic: earth, air, fire, and water. The tragedy played itself out on that invisible trajectory that knits together the earth and the heavens. This fiery chariot that left the sky and the sea blank and staring haunts us because it whispers to our own human depths of our nature and destiny.

Culture Two Catholics understand that there is no way to package mystery to make it more comprehensible or endurable. No five stages of mourning can ever be applied successfully to this occurrence, which, try as we might, we cannot wrap up in headlines, commission findings, or the platitudes of religions, which have forgotten that you cannot soothe or shout down mystery this immense. There is no way to solve spiritual challenges that awaken us to aspects of ourselves we have come near to forgetting altogether. Cost accounting does not apply to the sacramental events that shake the earth and sky. This is not something that can be prayed over platitudinously or regarded as only a scientific problem. The spiritually mature are not ashamed to feel unsettled, for they sense that something greater than we can measure or explain has touched us all. Some events are too great to be controlled; they have enormous spiritual authority that compels our attention. We will always hear the reverberations of genuine mystery in the depths of our beings. Perhaps that is what the porpoises symbolized for all of us, arching tenderly out of the water in one last signal about the depths of this mystery.

14

Finding the Grail

The Search for Credible Authority

Unity, not division, is our goal. Service, not power, is our mission. . . . In my cultural experience questioning is neither rebellion nor dissent. It is rather a desire to participate and is a sign of both love and maturity.
—Mrs. Donna Hanson, addressing Pope John Paul II
San Francisco, September 18, 1987

Pope John Paul II seemed weary as, near the end of his 1987 visit to the United States, he sat beneath the angled vaults of San Francisco's modern cathedral. Culture Two Catholicism stood just across the sanctuary, addressing him in the person of Mrs. Donna Hanson, mother of two sons and secretary for social ministry in the diocese of Spokane, Washington. In a high-intensity moment of truth this woman, neither rebel, heretic, nor "selective" believer, revealed herself as an adult, responsible, unapologetic Culture Two Catholic, who sought not to overturn but to serve the church.

The slightly squinting John Paul did not respond directly to this extraordinary woman, whose tone and insight bespoke her clear sense of being as much a part of the church as the pope himself. In those few memorable seconds, Culture Two looked directly into the frowning, uncertain face of Culture One. In that instant, Culture Two clearly confirmed itself in the richest sacramental sense, for it had clearly put away the things of a child and expected to be treated as an adult. In an unforgettable image, Culture One, embodied in the fatigued pope, expressed its institutional discomfort if not dismay. The institution did not know how to respond to this adult, peaceful, fully present woman, for it would not embrace her and could not transform her into a girl again. The organizational coils tensed and creaked ominously in that scene, only the most recent reenactment of a drama that has been repeated times beyond counting in the history of Catholicism. Culture One had found but failed to recognize the grail, suffering such inner constraint that it could not respond to this spiritual reality in a natural and healthy way. This awkwardness was reinforced during the Roman Synod on the Laity in the next month through the removal by papal decision of any meaningful opportunity to vote on resolutions expanding women's roles in the institutional church.

The institutional church thus lags behind but is very similar to other institutions in its contemporary dealings with women. In the reluctance to accept women as equals in the workplace or in the church, both business and ecclesiastical entities reveal an impacted machismo. At some as yet uncharted level, powerful men, by instincts as old and shadowed as history itself, resist the development of fully mature and reciprocal relationships with women. They may grant them improved conditions and opportunities but they seldom if ever allow them parity of opportunity, salary, or responsibility. It is always *yes, but.* Perhaps in no area does the Culture One church more obviously manifest its essential identity with secular institutions than in its deeply ingrained fear of grown-up women. Indeed, the institutional church may be the father of them all in this regard. The burden of this chapter, as suggested earlier, is to hold the lamp up to these long, crooked veins of anxiety about women that splay down the columns of institutional history, revealing the unattended flaws of the structure.

This is not a critique of the church as a sacrament to the world, a religious movement, or a way of life. These observations are raised to prompt a fresh and undefended exploration of the purely institutional dynamics that have played such a major role in shaping its character, especially in the centuries since the sixteenth-century Council of Trent. Powerful unnamed energies churn in the dark torrent of opposition to equal relationships with women. And this is related, psychologically speaking, to the instinctive desire to maintain a hierarchical organization in which all effective governance will rest with the top layers of the male clergy. The Counter-Reformation was marked by a sharp retrenchment from the Protestant positions that sharply questioned the need for this clerical level of ecclesiastical mediation between ordinary people and God. Valid theological questions were swept aside by the tidal-wave response, whose political motivation was centered on regaining effective control of the church as institution. Not all of these moves were made on the conscious level, for so deep are these impulses that they cannot be acknowledged except in the disguise of theological rationalization. This same need to regain centralized control of the institutional church has surfaced regularly since Vatican II, and on no occasions more clearly than Pope John Paul II's 1987 visit to the United States and the Roman Synod that followed in the next month.

Whatever the pope's intentions as an administrator in refurbishing his teaching authority over Culture Two Catholics during that trip, he had an effect far different and more mysterious than the one he proposed or expected. By appealing to the will and failing to ignite the imagination of mature Culture Two Catholics, Pope John Paul II unintentionally removed the harsh lines from papal imagery, lessening its imperial majesty by being less imperially majestic than popes, especially of the last century, seemed at a distance. He did not overwhelm, or speak in threatening tones, as he repeated Culture One assertions, such as "Women are not called to the priesthood," to Culture Two audiences. The pope was more the pastor saddened at the misunderstandings of his flock than the regent outraged by their behavior. His American listeners therefore did not react like subjects. While they respected and liked John Paul II as priest and man, they viewed him in a new and unprecedented manner, as one voice, even though a highly important one, among many raised on serious religious subjects.

John Paul graciously entered into carefully prepared dialogues with diverse representatives of American Catholicism as he journeyed across the continent. That he participated in these situations —allowing the pope to be perceived as a listener as much as a preacher—was far more significant in the long run than his immediate, perhaps weariness-inspired decision not to respond directly to the simple eloquence of Mrs. Hanson. By his manner and his mode of relationship to Americans the pope dimmed the regal aura that had been so blinding only a few generations before.

While John Paul attempted to call everyone back to a "vertical" (read *hierarchical*) model of Catholicism, the medium in which he did it was one of operational collegiality, of a pope in dialogue on serious matters at every point in his itinerary. And the medium in this case was far more significant than the message. The popes who succeed him will necessarily follow this fresh path of relationship with Catholics accustomed to a pope who speaks but listens, even if the actual dialogue has not been deeply or fully developed as yet. The pope cannot and will not be the distant figure on the unapproachable throne, for that is an image out of the past that has been operationally retired by the bold and journeying pope who belongs both to that past and to the future. Future popes, then, will remain at the center not just of the vastly deployed institutional church, Culture One, but of the church gathered as a people, a family eager for conversation, that is, Culture Two.

The 1987 papal journey to the United States turned out to be more mysterious, in the spiritual sense, than its planners could have anticipated. For, although their objective was to manage all communication within Culture One, the pope, through relating even hesitantly to it, was touched and affected by Culture Two, by the reality of a vital Catholicism outside institutional walls. The second culture was, in fact, confirmed in its existence and its beliefs about being the church through this journey. As *National Catholic Reporter* editor

Thomas Fox observed, "Such was not the purpose of this papal visit. But it is the product of it."* American Catholics felt an increased confidence in themselves and in American Catholicism in general. They developed a less than perfect yet experientially new relationship with the pope. He remains their father but they now see themselves as adults. One can expect that Culture One figures below the level of the pope will fight tenaciously to keep this kind of relationship from developing further. They want people to be dependent on the institution. More precisely, they want believers to be dependent on them. One may, therefore, see the pope's movement into dialogue as a shift that seeds the consciousness of the church, as a time-release medication does, for a steady movement away from the monarchical to the collegial style.

How much of this did the pope plan or recognize? He is far too shrewd not to understand the implications of these increasingly collegial visits around the world. Still, during the October 1987 synod, the protocol of monarchy was firmly in place, employed with almost palpable delight by loyalists, who emphasized inappropriately ornate papal language and the use of military metaphors to describe the institutional church. The mood of these bureaucratic underlings was faded twenties European, that of White Russians huddled together in Paris, bowing to each other's hollow crowns, murmuring dead titles as salutations, and talking of a restoration of czarist imperialism. As the world had changed permanently around them, so too it had around the Roman officials and specially favored groups, such as Opus Dei, which seem to construe the good news of Jesus as an elitist secret and themselves as crack, sworn troops, crusaders rather than seekers of the grail. Such groups may attempt to reestablish a monarchical Catholicism and may gain some Pyrrhic victories over the next decade. But crusaders cannot and will not survive the open country of the twenty-first century, the space age into which the rest of the world is inexorably moving.

One of the chief, as yet unfaced, conflicts of institutional Catholi-

*National Catholic Reporter, September 25, 1987, p. 40.

cism concerns human sexuality. With every effort to understand and forgive institutional foibles, it is impossible to ignore this awkward, unsettled business. Culture One has serious, deeply rooted difficulties with sexuality, especially with female sexuality. The institution does not readily admit the problem even to itself and, instead, insists on maintaining positions that advertise rather than mask the problem. It seems unable to die to itself in order to empty itself of historical distortions, thinking authoritarianism something to be clung to instead of surrendered for the sake of newer life. The conflict over certain questions connected with human sexuality is evident in the institution's determination to make its stand on issues that, viewed in a richer perspective, hardly justify Culture One's defensiveness about them.

Thus, the curialist oeuvre: birth control, the celibacy of priests, and the battle against women's entrance into the priesthood. Why have these issues become tests of loyalty to the Holy See as if they were critical articles of the creed? They are concrete, for one thing, and their common denominator is sex. Their salience in the consciousness of Roman authorities suggests either a conflicted obsession with these problems or an institutional reflex so deep as to be inaccessible to easy examination or recall. Organizational instincts seek mastery over this area in which people remain highly vulnerable and where techniques of shaming and ridicule can be used to best effect. The excessive resistance to the admission of women to the priesthood only makes the institutional argumentation against it more suspect and shaky. Why, one might ask, literally in God's name, must women be kept out of the priesthood, for which their natural gifts fit them so well?

The answer is not complicated. The institutional church keeps women out of the priesthood less from theological conviction than from psychological need to maintain and enhance masculine command of its ranks. The word *curia* is a mysterious revelation in itself. It derives from the Latin *co-vir,* which means *men together,* in short, male bonding at the highest level, the impulse to male aggregation as organizational nucleus for the cells of the institutional organism.

The organizational dimension of Catholicism may thus be deeply seeded with negative attitudes toward female equality and a skeptical reluctance to accept them in equal relationships. The hesitation of administrators even to admit the possibility of such motivation dooms the institution to defensive postures that will hasten the very results that its administrators fear, a reduction of their own credibility and a weakening of their claims to teaching authority.

Voices were raised from all over the world during the October 1987 Roman Synod, calling for an overdue proclamation of the equality of women in the church. The primate of Ireland, Tomás Cardinal O'Fiaich, underscored the universality of the concern by observing that concern for women was "not just an American aberration." Still, the official church seems very far from ever dealing with this profound pro-masculine prejudice within institutional Catholicism.

The obviously intense struggle between authoritarian elements of the male hierarchy and the rising voice of women aware of their dignity, equality, and ecclesial and pastoral abilities constitutes what psychology terms an unobtrusive measure of the larger problem of the search for healthy modes of authority within the Church. One can find, in the work of Professor Rudolph Bell, careful analyses of such measures of the institution's efforts to maintain control, particularly of women, throughout history. In *Saints and Society** Bell and his colleague trace the way the ecclesiastical process of making saints reflected the institutional church's reactions not only to the Reformation but to the threat of a general piety free of organizational supervision. "The early sixteenth century," they write, ". . . was a time of crisis for the cult of saints. Saints had embodied religious innovation and given direction to popular piety for the preceding three hundred years, but with the Reformation the traditional structures of belief and organization came under fire as never before."†

Protestantism was a danger because it eliminated the need for a

---

*University of Chicago Press, 1982, with Donald Weinstein.
†*Ibid.*, p. 189.

mediating church structure; saints, such as Francis of Assisi, spoke to the imagination of people, providing them with a way of holiness that lay outside strict ecclesiastical supervision. Indeed, some saw in St. Francis the fulfillment of the prophecy of Joachim of Floris, who, centuries before, had foreseen an era in which the church would shed its institutional structures for a new, freer mode of Christian life. The institution as institution could not long tolerate such frontal assaults on its close supervision of the Christian life.

"The response of the Counter Reformation church," Bell and Weinstein write, ". . . was to assume increasing control of cult formation and then to make it less accessible to popular and spontaneous religious enthusiasm." Control was important, they note, because "the saints challenged the clerical hierarchy on several fronts." Not only were their heroic lives a reproach to the clergy in general but also to the development of local cults, the "mongering of relics" that sometimes "set monasteries and towns against each other," as well as to the "local communes driving for autonomy (who) used cults of local saints to enhance their standing as well as to focus civic patriotism. Some of the more powerful, like Venice, even had pretensions to religious authority independent of and equal to that of the papacy."

The institutional church's response in quickly repositioning control into the hands of clerics had a number of negative effects on women. Not only were they severely limited in their aspirations within the church but their lives came ever more certainly under the control of men in an already patriarchal society. Combined with related cultural attitudes toward female sexuality and rigid societal roles and expectations, women were strongly and adversely affected by the Counter-Reformation. Even the number of declared male saints, from the sixteenth century on, rose enormously in comparison to that of women. This powerful, pervasive suppression of women in person, and their idealization in the abstract, have been aspects of institutional policy ever since. What women are now confronting in the institutional church is not some divinely ordered inequality but the consistent implementation of male-dominated organizational executive policies. This can never be dealt with success-fully until the institution at least begins to examine its own con-science on these matters.

The struggle has been engaged for centuries, but because of the strength of the masculine hold on the institutional church it has been carried out in a largely symbolic fashion. The unresolved nature of the effort by women to achieve equality and autonomy has had differing cultural incarnations, each of them revealing not only the changing societal climate but also the countervailing responses of the institution to maintain its control. At every juncture, however, they are linked dynamically to internal attitudes that the institution has misnamed for so long that it still cannot quite bring itself to address the true nature of its anti-woman prejudices. In a further work,* Bell has studied the varying styles of female sanctity, each a disguised striving for autonomy, throughout church history. He identifies the constantly developing modes of heroic holiness as the dynamic fe-male response to an ever-more-vigilant and steadily responsive male hierarchy's efforts to secure its control over women.

Extreme fasting, akin to today's anorexia, was employed by St. Catherine of Siena and St. Clare of Assisi, among hundreds of oth-ers, as their only way of escaping male clerical control and estab-lishing some autonomy of their own. Dominated by the male church and general culture in every other way, they could defy and frustrate confessors and ecclesiastical authority through con-trolling their own eating habits, their own bodies. This was a medieval prophecy for the functional uses of anorexia in our own day. Beneath the surface accidents, the struggle for individuality, for breaking the male ordering of their existences, was the true story of these women's lives. As Bell observes, "It . . . became evident that woman's holiness was the consequence of sacrifice and willpower; no longer could the female saint be viewed simply as the receptacle of divine grace, always in need of male guidance.

*Holy Anorexia, University of Chicago Press, 1985.

Woman as object, possessed of no interior spirituality, gave way to woman as subject, creator of her destiny."*

The Reformation, according to Bell, included an enormous reaction against this feminine claim to spiritual territory outside the control of what he calls a "hierarchical male prelacy." This, as we have observed, "meant a counterattack on the lay piety, with its emphasis on individual responsibility, that for three centuries since Bernard of Clairvaux and Francis of Assisi had flourished within mother church's bosom and that had now become its mortal enemy."† The subsequent massive efforts to control female spirituality by placing it once more firmly under the control of men led to a decline of fasting and, through the centuries, to the rise of fresh strategies on the part of women to free themselves from the reassertion of excessive masculine control. The succeeding styles of piety, which came at one point to include apparently bizarre forms of illness, exemplified by saints who spent most of their time in bed (and therefore outside control of their communities or church authority), are the crooked lines writing straight about women's continuing struggle to outwit or subvert male authority.

A further shift extended over the threshold of this century as female holiness found its expression in zeal for charitable works. Women effectively expressed their extraordinary capacity for independent achievement in running hospitals, schools, and carrying out other good works. Mother Cabrini has now been succeeded by Mother Teresa, who stands, ironically, as a symbol not of old ecclesiastical authority, as institutional leaders like to perceive her, but of women's ability to overcome its true authoritarian nature and to achieve spiritual and personal autonomy. Just as popes and bishops admired but feared holy women a thousand years ago, so they respect but are rendered powerless in the presence of Mother Teresa today. She supports church authority yet is able to stand independent

*Ibid., p. 150.
†Ibid., p. 151.

of it; it would be difficult, if not impossible, to imagine any pope, bishop, or monsignor telling her how, where, or when she should work. Mother Teresa is, in fact if not in her own consciousness, the best current example of a woman religious whose principal authority flows and is inseparable from her own person. She is an extraordinary feminist in a traditional religious habit.

The Nobel laureate nun is the free contemporary woman disguised in the habit of the old church, whose best traditions she serves even as she spurns and humbles its bureaucrats. It is not uncommon for Mother Teresa, for example, to arrive at a house prepared by some bishop or superior for use by her community and to dispose of the chosen rugs and furnishings, for her to assert, in short, that no man can or will decide the conditions of her apostolate. There is a hint of feminine assertion beneath the surface of her relationships with institutional leaders, and the latter, smiling gratefully if somewhat uneasily in photographs with her, accept her terms of service with an eagerness they display in relationship to nobody else. Do these worthies ever ask themselves why they must always accept her terms unconditionally in their negotiations with her? And how, despite her own demurrals, could anyone argue that a woman as spiritually remarkable as Mother Teresa is not really capable of being a priest, or, for that matter, the pope?

The present conflicted relationship between the church and women is but the latest episode in a long and difficult story. And today, as never before, women can and do operate independently of the asserted authority of the church. This mirrors the deep feelings of many Catholics, even quite traditional ones, who are spiritually autonomous, outside the reach of professional ecclesiastics. One familiar and long-revered form of the religious life is now collapsing not because of lack of faith but because its male-dominated structures no longer fit or provide healthy channels for the religious energies of modern women. So, too, the male-bonded culture of clerical life, which is always to be distinguished from the essence of priesthood, is close to ruin, not because of a lack of commitment to ministry, but because its cultural forms are vestiges of the great days of hierarchical preference and privilege, the pre-Copernican inheritance that was spent long ago.

The Roman Synod of 1987 will one day be perceived as the last dogged stand for the overly clericalized aspects of the church. It was, for Culture Two Catholics, an ambivalent, two-sided event. In short, a satisfactory mystery for those who could see beneath the lingering triumphalism, the royalist maneuvering, to its reality. The synod bore elements of past and future, of death and life, and the very halls in which it convened trembled because of fresh energies as much as ancient faults. This meeting, providentially on the subject of the laity, seemed to turn out as a complete triumph for steadfast curialists, for the *men together* who wanted to regain centralized, authoritarian regulation of the institutional church. At the synod's conclusion such men had successfully stifled for the moment, through effective silencing of the discussion, any expansion of women's participation in the church, although this was sought by bishops from all over the world. The synod seemed a strong victory for those forces whose vision of the church was of a hierarchical kingdom rising once again above the earth toward heaven.

In fact, these institutional churchmen, in looking backward, in turning away from the brightening light of the space age, in identifying the Promised Land as an authoritarian realm, have exiled themselves in the Waste Land instead. Their victory is an illusion, for they misunderstand themselves as badly as they misinterpret the millions of Catholics who identify themselves as the People of God, the church as a sacrament to the world, the church as the screen through which spiritual reality may be seen. The temporary advantage won by the curialists cannot be sustained in a world in which they cannot effectively implement their authoritarian vision without destroying it at the same time. Pope John Paul II, perceiving himself as a modern Paul, whose chief task, in journeying often, is to evangelize the world, has left the governance of the church largely to institutionalists, whose maneuvers will not in the long run serve his spiritual authority well. As this great leader continues to travel the globe, he will come gradually to realize that the era of monarchy has ended, that Catholics see and respond to him differently, that the future he resists is more powerful than the past he reverences. He will come to realize that he, too, is searching for the grail and that he will find it, as all must, in entering into instead of attempting to dominate the diverse mystery of the world.

This turning away on the part of large numbers of Catholics, Americans among them, from played-out institutional forms represents a search for healthy authority as much as a rejection of pathological authoritarianism. Culture One leaders must read the signs of these times accurately, for it is they, not their followers, who have failed to understand and express the healthy spiritual authority that, like the voice of the true shepherd, cannot be mistaken by the flock. To accomplish this, however, they must allow many purely organizational aspects of Culture One to undergo a transforming death. This will require them to lay aside their convictions that religion, ever the ambiguous mystery, whose native language is metaphor and symbol, can be expressed in terse, concrete, literal forms that weaken and ultimately destroy the meaning of faith. Culture One leaders need not know exactly what will rise to replace the institutional forms that no longer serve well. They can have confidence that, if they trust the healthy instincts of healthy people, these forms will develop organically and will serve the church as a collegial people well into the next century. This requires a profound act of faith on their part. First, they must believe that death can lead to resurrection. Second, they must seek to be generative, bearers of true authority, rather than controllers, or agents of authoritarianism.

The members of Culture Two, the real church as People of God, have understood this for a long time.

15

Where God Is Homeless, and We All Are at Home

To an open house in the evening
Home shall men come,
To an older place than Eden
And a taller town than Rome;
To the end of the way of the wandering star,
To the things that cannot be and that are,
To the place where God was homeless
And all men are at home.
　　　　　—G. K. Chesterton, "The House of Christmas"

Too late have I loved you, O Beauty so ancient yet ever new. Too
late I loved you! And, behold, you were within me.
　　　　　—St. Augustine, *Confessions X, 27*

The future enters into us, in order to transform itself in us, long
before it happens.
　　　　　—Rainer Maria Rilke, *Letters to a Young Poet*

Not the least of the ironies of the present position of Catholics in
America is that its bishops have gained attention and respect in the
public forum just as the institutional culture that they oversee has

begun a natural and ineluctable decline. Large numbers of American Catholics have attained fine educations and acceptable and honorable places in American society; they have also gained a degree of theological understanding beyond any imagining of it by the immigrant forebears whose dedication to, and generous sacrifices for, the institutional church made the ascendancy of the present generation of Catholics possible. And in this very moment of achievement these same Catholics are moving steadily out of the shadow of the looming institution, looking back as longing exiles do, hoping for, yet despairing of receiving, the deep sacramental, spiritual response that will call them back from their outward journey. The air is empty and silent, the fortress church recedes on the horizon, and these Catholics continue their quest, conscious of themselves as a people rather than subjects of a sovereign organization. They are Catholics outside the walls of the institution, whose leaders speak with less authority to their lives every day.

In many ways, of course, nothing seems to have changed in the American Catholic Church. Despite the transformations that have delighted some and dismayed others since Vatican II, its main elements remain the same. People are going to church, getting married and being buried; bishops wear their medieval regalia, conduct meetings, and, indeed, are attracting wider attention than they have received since their first convocation in revolutionary times. So far, the shrinkage in Mass attendance, vocations, parishes and schools, have been regarded as acceptable losses. And yet, just as on the longest of summer days the earth is turning steadily toward autumn, so the shadows of the institutional church's magnificent towers are lengthening as it bends into a new season. "There is no cure for Autumn," wrote John Cheever, "no medicine for the north wind." And, one might add, no postponing the continuing change that, seemingly resisted mightily on the conscious level of organizational church life, is at work deep within it, ripening out of the seeds of the future adrift on the solar wind.

The institution and the people are moving at a constant rate away from each other, their identities as distinct cultures of Catholicism becoming more obvious every day. Culture Two feels that it is becoming more of a church and less of an institution, while Culture One concentrates on being more of an institution, husbanding and consolidating itself, yet, in an utterly practical way, preparing itself for inevitable changes. In large institutions, however, the right hand often does not acknowledge what the left is doing. Thus, for example, even in large Catholic dioceses such as Baltimore and Chicago, one reads of plans for what are termed "pastoral alternatives," that is, parishes headed by laypersons, ordinarily religious women, as responses to the shortage of priests. Such experiments have already taken place in many smaller United States dioceses, and are not uncommon throughout the world.* That the institution is well along in adjusting to the future is proven by the fact that these changes have risen from the realm of theory to that of bureaucratic planning. "Diocesan policy now exists," we read, recognizing a familiar tone, "to provide for the orderly appointment of pastoral administrators." If you want to read the future, pay attention to the level of behavior, for it is what people actually *do,* rather than what they *say,* that offers our best prediction of things to come.

These adjustments, for all their apparent smallness, are significant because they affect the main setting for the religious experience of Catholics, the parish and its sacramental life. This is, then, a poignant moment, for beneath the faded titles of monarchy the institutional church is, in fact, still reactive to its environment. And it remains in possession of the resources that, effectively used, could respond to the spiritual needs of the world and, in particular, of Culture Two Catholics, while also promoting what it desperately needs—its own healthy, organic growth into less regal forms. The greater part of these treasures is not found, of course, in Culture One's conscious, rational administrative existence, but in its rich unconscious life. These unnumbered treasures include sacramental intuitions, a recoverable native language of symbol and ritual, and a long, intimate knowledge of the human heart, of sin and forgiveness; add, too, the

*Cf. *The Chicago Catholic,* January 8, 1988, p. 3.

hard-bought wisdom and understanding won in long vigils with human beings, a certain battered comfort with the ironic, the para-doxical, the mysterious. If ever there was a church capable of being a home for human beings, it is that church, that reality still breathing beneath hierarchical tombs and monuments.

Another resource is one more readily understood by administra-tors, for, although the collegial process bears, as branch does bud, a profound theological truth about generative authority, it also matches their capacity for and familiarity with meetings and their countless offspring of minutes, resolutions, and future agendas. Col-legiality acknowledges the authority each bishop holds in his own right as a shepherd and allows for wide participation by all Catholics in public meditations on the application of the gospel in their daily lives. This vehicle permits the church to let the stiff trappings of its lost royal history drop from its shoulders and to feel lighter and freer for it. Thus unburdened, the church can rediscover within itself a profound and plangent spiritual authority. Collegiality makes room for healthy debates and for the wholesome development of new forms of pastoral presence.

Collegiality has already proven itself as a process, and it has been employed in ways that have expanded and deepened people's spiritual concerns in, for example, tasks as varied and significant as the development of pastoral letters on nuclear war and the economy as well as in the resolution of major conflicts, such as that over Archbishop Hunthausen in Seattle. Authoritarian settlements, which by nature are imposed without discussion and sometimes without any apparent grasp of the theological issues involved, as in the case of Catholic University's Charles Curran, have proven disastrous. Collegiality will, despite widespread criticism of it by curialists in the present, provide the church with a sensible, measured way of grow-ing and of recovering healthy spiritual authority.

Indeed, as institutional resources continue to decline, the sacra-mental heart of Catholicism appeals to and stabilizes Culture Two Catholics in their fundamental religious identity. The sacramental, far more than the administrative, responses of the church are the river of spiritual energy that flows from the deep, hidden wellsprings of Culture One into Culture Two. The connections are not papal or episcopal as much as they are symbolic and sacramental. The celebration of the Eucharist, as has been observed, exerts a strong pull on Catholics who identify it as *the* reason for their maintaining a connecting spiritual identity with the institution that in other ways neither inspires or attracts them. The sacraments are the binding strength of the church's ministries, innervating them everywhere, especially in those carried out in extraordinarily multiplied settings by laypersons. Where clerics are no longer present, Catholics convene around the essentials of their faith, often under the leadership of religious women, as the development of current ecclesiastical policy validates. These services include scriptures, prayers, and the distribution of the Eucharist. As we observe these successful ministries—especially those free of excessive bureaucratic regulation—we also discover the aspects of the Catholic tradition that speak effectively to human spiritual needs.

In the history of the church in countries like Japan, just such services have preserved the faith during long priestless generations. They will increasingly do so in America's Catholic Church as we draw closer to the next century. As the scepters and orbs of the monarchical era fall gently into their resting places in museum and memory, the essentials of Christian worship will stand out with great clarity. Rooted in and reflective of the sacramental system, the occasions of the community's celebration will coincide with the cycle of human needs to which the sacraments are already keyed—to birth and growth and love and illness and death, to the story the moon tells us every month about the intersections of mystery at which, sooner or later, we all meet. One need not be a prophet to understand that the organic growth of Catholicism in the next century depends on generously, if not prodigally, reinforcing these strengths rather than arguing such discredited theses as that women are ontologically unfit for the priesthood.

All significant readings taken of the mentality of curialists suggest that they seek a consolidation of power in Rome in the Promised

Land of their own limited viewpoint. But these men can no longer automatically control the consciences or beliefs of their people and cannot effectively force on them a literalist theory and practice of religion in an age in which human beings are searching for a faith that understands and celebrates the dappled mysteries of ordinary existence. The efficacy of control is doomed in a world in which it is impossible to contain or shape the flow of information. The truth still makes men and women free. The institutional insistence on a return to nineteenth-century ways, at which time the control of information was relatively easy, merely accelerates the disintegration of the curialist claims to authority and hastens the departure of good people from its spiritual jurisdiction. But they do not want to go, and would not if church leaders emphasized their pastoral, sacramental, rather than institutional roles.

Absent some conversion of heart on the part of institutionalists, the future of these two cultures is not difficult to read. Culture Two is well past listening, much less responding, to leaders who, when the chips are down, emphasize institutional loyalty above all else. There are many good men among the bishops who, by their every experience of training, selection, and ambition, will go with the organization on every issue. Extraordinary bishops exist throughout the world who understand this problem very well. Their strategy is to remain loyal to the institution while buying time and creating space in which it will be able to grow organically in the next century. This is an enormously difficult position for them to occupy as the central church administration continues its plan of filling the ranks of the episcopate around them with confirmed loyalists.

Many elements of institutional identity that are wonderfully colorful and familiar will have to die before the structural church can renew itself as a true *sacramentum mundi*. Its leaders, as noted, presently demonstrate no inclination to examine themselves or the structure that, in its darkest soul, has been so profoundly and consistently prejudiced against women. They speak of continuing "a dialogue" with women. But, as one Culture Two Catholic woman observed,

"For today's bishops, 'dialogue' is a weapon to keep us under control while not taking us seriously."

As Culture Two Catholics move away from the institutional parameters of Catholicism they will not abandon completely their deep affection for their faith and for its genuine sacramental authority. Such Catholics will respond to the living elements of the faith in those parishes where they do shine forth unmistakably. The official institution, however, *as an institution,* is likely to count itself relieved that they have gone or at least moved away from its center. Culture One, like a great multinational corporation, is not without strategic resources. The institution may, as many of its administrators already have mistakenly done, write off the West, especially the United States, as spiritually flabby and morally decadent and will turn its attention to the Third World. There it sees a rich harvest of new Catholics better prepared to embrace and identify with traditional church structures. In short, such bureaucratic leaders expect Third World Catholics, particularly those on the African continent, to be more receptive of their authority and more amenable to their control. This grand design ignores the message delivered by bishops from throughout the world at the 1987 Roman Synod. These local churches are not naïve, nor are they lacking in curiosity, spiritual sensitivity, or an awareness that it is the church as a sacrament rather than an organization that inspires their loyalty and their commitment to the dissemination of gospel principles in their own countries.

The priests and religious men and women who function in the Third World are also, after all, far more theologically sophisticated than they have ever been. They are keenly aware of the desperate needs of their people, and in many places their pastoral practices are far less under the control of Rome than officials would like to believe. Not in vain did the late German Jesuit theologian Karl Rahner once speculate on the possibility of the development of varying moral systems that respected the long-term traditions of Third World countries. He challenged the Roman institutional domination of moral thinking by asking, "Must the marital morality of the Masai in East Africa be that of Western Christianity? Or could a chieftain there, even if he is a Christian, live in the style of the patriarch Abraham?" Such a question placed by perhaps the most influential Catholic thinker of the twentieth century suggests the seeds of inquiry that have already germinated and grown to harvest worldwide in a new generation of theologians.

The vast continents that are materially underdeveloped are not necessarily spiritually underdeveloped and, although they are growing ecclesially at disparate paces, they are not going to fall in place and cede their traditions to Roman control easily. Their dynamic growth, flowing from sources other than the controversies born in Western Europe five hundred years ago, will not pivot on questions, such as the reaffirmation of celibacy, that have been worn threadbare by the keening winds of time. These issues, so deeply a part of the consciousness of the institutionalists who identify the church with the cultural history of Western Europe, are not of great import to Catholics in the Third World. They will ignore them, push them aside, as they inquire about the issues that are urgent to them—about the fundamentals of justice, poverty, and the opportunity for a non-Westernized Christianity that does not subvert but accepts their own spiritual traditions.

The church, as first sensed by Pope John XXIII at the dawning of the space age, will become more truly universal and less European, and the changes wrought in it by the new age will make the minor transformations of Vatican II seem like trifles. Culture One may be clutching its imperial robes about itself because it already feels the chill of the unknown, the cold breeze of the mystery of death and resurrection to its antiquated forms that it will inevitably experience in the next century. It holds more tightly to Rome as the pulsating center of orthodoxy because at some level of consciousness this institutional culture realizes that it must let go of this center in the horizonless new age, in which the center can be anywhere. Indeed, the demand of the space age is that the Catholic Church die to the institutional forms and practices that, in its cathedrals and traditions, seem eternally begotten as the durable foundation stones of an everlasting structure.

That the European heritage of Catholicism may be transformed is the inevitable outcome of any authentic ecumenical movement. The working out of the details of a coming together of the great churches of East and West will be hastened by the new environment of space. *Ecumenical* comes from the Greek *oikoumenikos,* of the whole world. *Oikein* means to inhabit, and *oikos* means house. The root *weik* links a familiar group of words, including *diocese, ecology, economy,* and *parish.* These notions meld in the space age, for the great insight of our journey into the stars allows us to see that we belong to one family and that we live in the same house.

What is striking about the journey into space is precisely the view that it gives of our world. From the vantage point of space, wrenched out of our certainty that we sit at the center of all things, we perceive the universe afresh. As Joseph Campbell has written of the famous photograph of earthrise taken from the moon, "Is the center the earth? Is the center the moon? The center is anywhere you like. Moreover, in that photograph from its own satellite, the rising earth shows none of those divisive territorial lines that on our maps are so conspicuous and important. The Holy Land is no special place. It is every place that has ever been recognized and mythologized by any people as home."*

The destiny of the churches, including that of the Catholic, is to pursue what unites rather than divides them. Perhaps the twentieth century has been filled with the anguished ethnic claims of people insisting on their rights over against each other as last gasps of a deadly understanding of ourselves that has dominated our imaginations for as long as we can remember. Perhaps the observed narcissism, the mirroring and much-mirrored self-centeredness of the late twentieth century, has been a last unconscious reaction to surrender-

*The Inner Reaches of Outer Space, New York, Alfred Van Der Marck Editions, 1986, p. 44.

ing our place at the center of everything. No small adjustment awaits us in this new century, but it is already being anticipated, not only by Culture Two Catholics as they venture forth in search of the spiritual reality beneath all realities, but in every human movement from the economic to the poetic, based on the steadily growing awareness of our interrelatedness. At the bottom of it all, as we recognize that the concretized religions, with their centuries of arguments and warfare over literal interpretations of spiritual truths, have lost their power to control our ideas of religion, we will speak again in metaphor, the natural language of faith and belief, and like the sightless and speechless in the scriptures, we will find our spiritual senses unbound.

When people ask about the meaning of their lives, they sometimes seem to want a linear, rational account that makes logical sense to them of the seemingly blind alleys and broken moments that they and their loved ones encounter regularly. But organized religion provides such explanations only at the risk of mocking itself, or of speaking in the superficial clichés that, as on the occasion of the *Challenger* disaster, reveal uneasiness with, or a lack of confidence in, spiritual depth. One cannot make sense out of the death of innocent children or the triumph of injustice in simplistic pieties that make those who speak them feel better but seldom touch those who are suffering.

In fact, religion does not explain life so that every little happening makes logical sense. At its truest, faith, and the organizations that symbolize it, provide a way of looking at the world that enables the suffering and the aggrieved to perceive its essential, nonrational characteristic of mystery. Religion reveals and explores, but does not conquer, the utter mystery that lies at the very root of existence. A sacramental church is meant to be a screen through which, by means of metaphor and symbol, people can penetrate the outer texture of every day and see into its radiant and ever-mysterious heart. The charge of a sacramental church is, in William Blake's words, to cleanse "the doors of perception." Meaning is delivered, not to those who master and control every instance of life, but to those who sense and experience the redemptive nature of its ordinary rhythms, to those, in other words, who do not shield themselves from the light and heat of mystery.

Those who feel that people are not prepared for the revelation of the ordinary, and that they need concise, clear answers handed down by distant religious authority figures, are inattentive to the spiritual restlessness of American culture. The New Age Movement, for example, is only the latest in a long series of pseudo-spiritual enterprises that have succeeded in America precisely because of the widespread longing for some spiritual interpretation of existence. According to reporter Richard Blow, perhaps 10 percent of Americans have opted for this religionlike pursuit that, under the leadership of Shirley MacLaine, features "channeling," or conversations through mediums with long-dead spirits, and the belief that crystals cure diseases and transmit thoughts.* That such profit-making nonsense should prove attractive to so many is a touching measure of the spiritual impoverishment of contemporary America.

The Catholic Church, less as an institution than as a sacrament to the world, can feed the religiously hungry, the mystery-starved people who are the immigrants of this century, ready to make any journey to find a Golden Door. But the genuine sacramental pilgrimage brings not answers but more profound questions. It delivers, however, a rich sense that, illogical or not, what we experience is what makes us human and transfigures us spiritually. The future of the church depends more on its recovery of its sacramental feeling for the world than on its institutional skills. For its main task is to provide a sacramental vision that grasps compassionately and insightfully what James Joyce described as "all that is grave and constant" in our condition.

There is no structural change, then, that cannot be dreamed of as long as such a transformation makes it possible for the church to carry out this pastoral mission to the world. The church must, of course, allow itself to hear and to speak in a spiritual vocabulary, in

*"Moronic Convergence," *The New Republic,* January 25, 1988, p. 24.

that "entirely new language," as it is described on the feast of Pentecost. That is not, we might note, the same as becoming charismatic. It means something much simpler and much less spiritually elitist. When the leaders of the institutional church can speak, for example, of the Virgin Birth as more than a historical fact—when they can realize that historicity is *not* the point—they will automatically enjoy again the spiritual teaching authority that has diminished so in our day. When they are able to appreciate that the metaphor of the Virgin Birth trails an aura of spiritual substance that is its primary significance, they will not lack for hearers.

In the lexicon of the soul, the Virgin Birth refers to the ideal of a life that is motivated not by wealth, power, or pleasure, but by values that transcend temporal survival. It is, therefore, a metaphor signifying the life urged on all by the Christian tradition and supported by the sacramental system. When religious leaders can speak of the Promised Land or Earthly Paradise as spiritual metaphors rather than as geographical locations, people's hearts will be opened to the primary religious reality that they symbolize. For the Promised Land, as Campbell describes it, "is any landscape recognized as mythologically transparent, and the method of acquisition of such a territory is not by prosaic physical action, but poetically, by intelligence and the method of art; so that the human being should be dwelling in the two worlds simultaneously of the illuminated moon and the illuminating sun."*

Culture Two Catholics seek and will confer authority on leaders who can open their eyes to the spiritual dimensions of the experiences that persons have every day. These vary widely but there is *no* human activity that is spiritually neutral. A man and woman in love may feel the earth move and, wanting to share everything with each other, sense something about the God beyond names who wants to share everything with them. The seemingly self-absorbed young person, educated to the consumer life, toting gym bag, packaged natural-food salad, and video cassette at day's end back to an empty apartment, is

*Campbell, p. 62.

not the achieving narcissist, not a figure of smug fulfillment as much as a touching incarnation of the isolation and loneliness, so deep that no echoes rise from its crevasse, of people who have been denied access to their own spiritual depths. They, too, would respond to those who could redeem their yearning for them.

No day passes without some opportunity for the church to point symbolically to the mysterious texture of life, to the possibilities of Virgin Births and entrances into Promised Lands all about us. The *Challenger* disaster was such an occasion, as we have already observed. But the commonplace images, each luminously sacramental, of the gospel rise before people constantly. Their sacramentality needs to be underscored so that men and women recognize that the great spiritual mysteries may be remembered inside church but they are celebrated in the seemingly homely daily round of events. A small child, for example, falls down a drainpipe and, through the media, the entire nation's attention is fixed on her plight. This incident contained all the elements of a Biblical epiphany.

For not only were the child's parents very youthful and poor, as Joseph and Mary were thought to be, but the child, finally rescued, recapitulated the mystery of every child restored to life in the gospels. The spiritual richness of this "miracle," in which modern machinery—the wonders of the human imagination—played no small part, lay, however, in the genuine revelation about the men and women who so unself-consciously joined in the rescue effort. For in those long hours, in a vigil of uncertain waiting to match those that arise in everyone's life, we were able to penetrate the everyday appearance of the people whose hearts were opened by the small girl's plight. We could see the goodness, the generosity, the self-effacement, the spiritual depth of ordinary people just doing, as so many of them said, "what they would do for anybody." And so we could see into our own selves more deeply as well. No channeling, no crystals, no permission from the bishop needed. The doors of perception were cleansed in that interval before the holiday season in which we were all born pure again and in which we could name that homely place of danger and rescue as the Promised Land.

That is but one example of the Spirit, "with ah! bright wings," hovering over our world. That is what people are looking for and, indeed, have a right to expect from their religious leaders—sacramental insight more than moralistic regulations. The future of Culture One depends on its understanding of this challenge and on its willingness to allow some of its institutional aspects to die so that it, too, can be born again in forms that enable it to reveal to the world the meaning of its suffering and hope. That is what Paul meant when he spoke of the whole of creation groaning in travail until now. If the leaders of Culture One listen carefully, they will hear it, too.

Index